Healing
YOUR MAP

A Guide to Understanding
Discernment, Trauma, and
Human Behavior

JODEE GIBSON, MA | PCC

Human Behavior Architect™
www.JodeeGibson.com
BIRMINGHAM, MICHIGAN

Healing Your Map: A Guide to Understanding
Discernment, Trauma and Human Behavior

ISBN: 979-8-9868969-2-2 (Trade Paperback)

ISBN: 979-8-9868969-7-7 (eBook)

LCCN Number: 2022917434

Penny Roberts, Cover Illustrator

First Edition

Printed in U.S.A.

Disclaimer: Please note that all information in this book is provided for educational purposes only and should not replace medical and/or psychiatric advice. The use of this book implies your acceptance of this disclaimer. If you wish to use *Healing Your Map* in the teaching of others, you are required to undergo the appropriate training and certification. Please visit www.jodeegibson.com for details.

To Mr. Francis Yezbick,
my HFCC English professor,
who took a chance on me.
Without you sir, this book would
not have been possible.
Your presence in my life forever
changed the trajectory of it.

Contents

PART I—The Map & The Territory

PART II—The Key to Your Map

PART III—Healing Your Map

Introduction

Imagine a book that leads you deep inside the journey of how you became you. Not a book that shares how you are supposed to be or labels you or makes any attempt to *fix* you. Simply a book that allows you to understand the inner workings of you and how it all was created. This book is about healing versus treating. It's about identifying and healing the roots versus treating the symptoms that emanate from them.

My belief is that awareness creates access. As the brilliant Dr. Maya Angelou often shared, people who know better, do better. Yet how can we be expected to do better if we don't have the access or the awareness to know the difference? If this concept speaks to you, this book was written for you.

As you journey through this book, allow yourself the time and space to explore. It was not written or designed to be read from cover to cover in one day. It was instead created as a tool, a reference and a resource guide to be used as needed. With the knowledge you will gain from this book, the future version of you simply becomes a few decisions away. The more transparency you allow, the more healing you will experience.

The world you can unlock with the information provided in this book is limitless. Here are a few things that are possible, once you master the content shared in this book.

➤ Heal your relationship with yourself

➤ Heal a relationship with another person

➤ Release old childhood memories that hinder your ability to thrive

➤ Learn to manage your emotions, removing the deep emotional responses that take you off track

➤ Hone your natural talents

➤ Change character traits that no longer serve you

➤ Step into that version of you that you often dream about

➤ Experience emotional freedom

➤ Achieve your lifelong dreams

You have no idea what you are capable of learning, doing or being once you step away from your old story and start healing your map. The time for change is now. It doesn't matter where you started, what matters is what you're willing to learn in order to heal.

PART I

The Map & The Territory

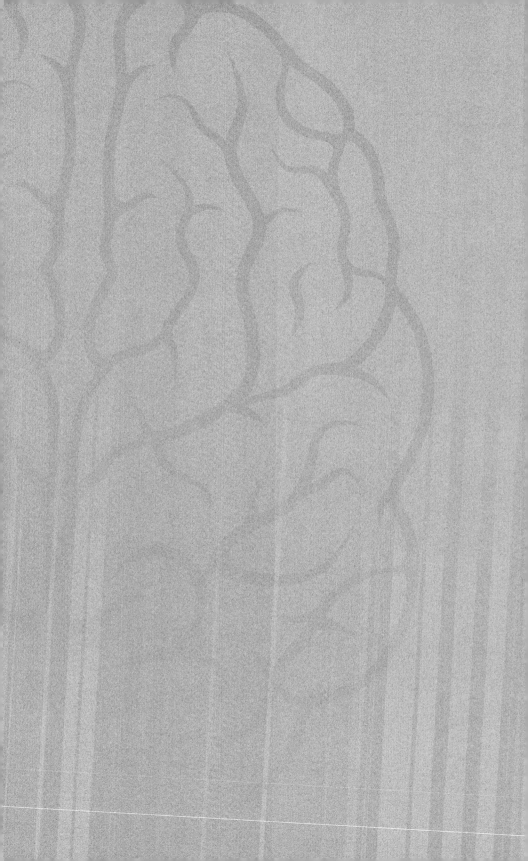

Chapter 1

The Map Is Not the Territory

As you open the door, it immediately smacks you in the face. The smell. It's that smell again. The smell that is embedded in every fiber of your being. That sterile, "I can identify that smell anywhere" kind of smell. It strikes every cell of your body, and it immediately paralyzes you. You don't know where it's coming from, and all you want is for it to stop because the more you inhale the more it takes you back. You can see the overhead lights. You can hear the machines. You can feel yourself laying on the cold, hard gurney as panic filled the room. There was beeping, machines alarming, frenetic noises. The smell invades your nostrils. It evokes the most visceral feeling you have ever experienced. You barely remember the accident, yet every ounce of your body knows that it happened.

That smell immediately transports you back to when you were seven years old. You were innocently riding your bike when that car came out of nowhere. You never even saw it. You have vague, patched-together stories told more from other people's perspectives than from your own memory. The stories are told with heightened emotion, and although you were the one on the bike, your ability to recall that day, and the four days that followed, has been erased from your memory—until that smell arrives. In those few and far in-between moments, your entire neurology is spoken for. How does this happen? How does your neurology store this content? Where does this reaction or smell live? And why does it only hijack your neurology?

If you've been searching for the answers to similar questions, this book is your guide. We'll explore answers to questions like:

> ➢ How can something be so unconsciously embedded into my being?

> ➢ How can something from so long ago still impact me so deeply?

> ➢ How can I have so many words yet am unable to speak?

> ➢ How can I have so many ingenious ideas yet still feel so stuck?

> ➢ How can I dream so big yet play so small?

If any of these questions resonate, keep reading. Have you ever wondered how it's possible that you can witness the same event with another person, yet walk away with completely different interpretations of what happened? The person you shared that moment with has a completely different recollection of what occurred. Their recollection may even take you aback. You look at them in complete disbelief, thinking that is *not* what happened! You may even be nervous in the moment to verbalize your disconnect, which leaves you so perplexed you remain silent. How can your perspectives differ so greatly? How is it possible that we all exist in the same territory, yet we all experience it so differently?

You, me and every single other human on this planet are all taking life in through the same five (and often six) senses. We smell things. We taste things. We feel things. We see things. And we hear things. And depending upon how calm our energy is on any given day, we may even experience moments when we intuitively *just know* things. Even though we are all taking the world in with the same senses, we all have extremely different recollections of what we experienced. So how does this happen?

Allow me to share a simple theory: **the map is not the territory**.

Take a moment and grasp the concept that a map is simply an interpretive tool used to navigate the territory you are experiencing. The map is not the actual territory. It's just the tool used to create perspective, calculate movement and orient you around the territory. Whether the map is on your phone, printed out from your computer or purchased at your local store, it's still just an interpreted model of the territory you experience. Think of it like your family portrait. The portrait captures the essence of who your family was at the moment the picture was taken. That physical picture is not the actual people. The actual people are either moving about this Earth or resting somewhere in peace. Whether they still reside in your household or they have grown up and moved on, the picture serves as a representation of that time and space. The picture is not the actual people in much the same way that the map is not the territory.

The Map

The map is simply the map. It's an independent, subjective tool unknowingly created to help you navigate and to keep you safe and out of harm's way. It makes complete sense if this feels a bit abstract right now. Embrace the idea that each one of us was born with a blank map. You were born with a map. I was born with a map. Each of us was born with a completely blank map. Each of our respective maps have been collecting and recording each and every moment of our lives, and they will continue to do so. Your map records your life. My map records my life. Each person's map records and encodes every single moment of each respective person's life.

You have a map.

Your siblings have a map.

Your kids have a map.

Your parents have a map.

Your spouse has a map.

Your boss has a map.

The clerk at your favorite store has a map.

Every single person on this planet has their own map.

My entire life's work came full circle when I first heard the statement *the map is not the territory*. I had just begun studying NLP (neuro linguistic programming) and my mind nearly exploded. These six amazing words "the map is not the territory" were first uttered by Alfred Korzybski. Korzybski was a linguist who lived deep inside the world of semantics. Although Korzybski's statement gave a brief glimpse into the world of semantics, it forever expanded my mind. For me, those six words immediately built an entire model in my head. The map is not the territory means that there is a map and there is a territory; they are two separate and independent spaces.[1]

Those six words gave meaning to a concept I had yet to grasp. They connected dots for me that had always been outliers. As someone who has spent the past three decades learning about personal development and self-mastery, they made something that previously felt so abstract immediately tangible. Isolating and identifying these two spaces forever changed my view of the world.

My Map, My Story

The map was simply a map. This concept explained the idea that it was not me that was in my way. It was not my perspective or my brokenness that was keeping me outside of my goals. It was my map—my wildly outdated, unhealthy map—that was creating the displaced effect. The concept of the map itself created space between how I felt and how I experienced the world. Before this awakening, I was incredibly stuck yet incredibly determined. The concept of the map and the territory immediately dismantled my old beliefs, creating space to build new ones. I had spent decades learning multiple disciplines on different ways to heal, and then it all came full circle. Those six words allowed me to grasp the concept that it was simply my map. My internal, highly subjective, and personalized map represented and housed my beliefs, and my map and my beliefs were wildly different from the actual territory—reality.

What I learned at that moment was that my internal world (my beliefs) dictated what I observed in my external world (actual reality). Beliefs versus reality. Korzybski's idea behind the statement was founded on the principle that beliefs and reality are two completely different things. Beliefs are the map. Reality is the territory. All that leads to the idea that although you believe one thing, the reality of that space can be much different from your belief.

Think about the last time your eyes landed on a delectable looking snack and how certain you were about the story your eyes told you. "This looks amazing," they said. Yet that story was far from the truth. As soon as that bite hit your tastebuds, your belief changed. It tasted terrible. Belief versus reality. Map versus territory. The same principle applies in those moments when you believe you are just going to run in the store and grab one thing, only to walk out thirty minutes later with multiple items and $100 less in your pocket.

Belief → I only need one thing. ← **Map**
Reality → Oh, but this is so cute. ← **Territory**

This concept, the map is not the territory, houses the way you unknowingly and unconsciously interpret and assimilate information in your world. Your map creates your very own personalized perspective. Throughout this book, you will gain an understanding that your beliefs are continually built from your very own, highly personalized map, while reality remains the standalone, objective territory you exist in.

Your map is what generates the perspective from which you experience the territory.

Dissecting this statement just a bit more reveals that your map represents your perspective of the territory, not the actual territory. Your map is a subjective space that has been built over time, and it is a direct reflection of all the things you've previously experienced and are now pulling into perspective from your present-day map.

Your Experience

Your map has been collecting and compiling content for decades. As shared above, your map records every single thing you have ever experienced in your entire lifetime. Every emotion. Every smell. Every taste. Every sound. Every color. Every face. Every person. It even captures and houses the things that you have completely forgotten about. Every single thing. It's all encoded onto your map. Although you may rarely have conscious awareness or recollection of much of your map's content, it still exists on your map. Know that each and every memory has the capacity to lie dormant on your map, consciously or unconsciously, for the rest of your life until it is again triggered.

Your map records rich, in-depth memories that tell past stories and create future ones. Most of the things recorded on your map were captured without your awareness, yet regardless of that lack of awareness, your map consistently collects content at a highly unconscious rate. Everything that has occurred prior to this exact moment has unknowingly been recorded on your map. The same is true for every other person's map.

Every event, every memory, every feeling and every thought has been recorded and encoded onto your map. Your map holds it all, even the things you believed you had left in the past. It houses your stories, your thoughts, your triumphs, your failures and every single emotion that has ever passed through your being. These events forever live somewhere on your map. Layers and layers of this content have been embedded together, now functioning at an incredibly normalized rate. These recordings lie dormant until they are triggered by unbeknownst stimuli.

You unconsciously use this exact map every single day to navigate through your life. Your map becomes the lens through which you experience the territory. Knowing what you have learned thus far, imagine how many different lenses people are using to experience the territory. It is endless, yet it all makes so much sense. Each of our maps houses our very own story and builds the perspective that we experience every day. Regardless of whether you have zero siblings or ten siblings and you were all raised in the same house with the same parents, you all have different maps. Your map has content that overlaps, yet each one of you will still have your very own, completely different, highly subjective, personalized maps. Even if you have an identical twin, you will still have two separate and distinct maps. Each person has their own respective map.

Over time, your subjective familiarity with your map allows you, and every other person on the planet, to normalize the things you experience. My map houses my story and builds the perspective that I normalize. Your map houses your story and the perspective you normalize. Your friend's map houses their story, so on and so forth. Because each one of our maps vary, each different map creates a different perspective. Due to each person's unique perspective, we each normalize different things. None of them are right or wrong; they are all just different. In these highly normalized spaces, our stories will vary, as each of us is technically correct. We go on to use these maps for all our decision-making. We use our map to navigate, to make decisions, to establish boundaries, to choose a direction, to determine intensity, to understand others and essentially to thrive and survive. Our maps are essentially our very own personalized GPS.

The variation in what we normalize creates the variation in perspective. And as you begin to understand your map, its meaning and its function, you can create utter clarity and awareness around how and why you perceive things in the way you do. Your map explains to you why you make the decisions you make, why you have the beliefs that you have and how it all ties together. That self-awareness alone creates more access than ever before. That powerful awareness then opens space, allowing you the opportunity to self-discover your patterns, your beliefs and the story that built them.

That was a great deal of content so allow me to pause. We're already diving into maps, perspectives and beliefs. I will completely unpack and disassemble all these pieces as we move through this book. My greatest intention for this book is that it becomes a tool and a reference source that allows you to simply create new awareness—the kind of awareness that leads to your ability to create the life you have always dreamed of. And with that new, deepened awareness, you will be able to fully understand your map, the maps of the people around you and the skills needed to influence both.

The more you know about your map, the more you begin to understand that things are not right or wrong. They are simply different—different from your map, different from what exists on someone else's map. Just different. This awareness creates more tolerance, more understanding and more empathy, which in return creates less judgment and less separation. The more you understand your map, the more you start stepping away from blame and judgment and start stepping into curiosity and understanding. It widens your perspective. You start embracing the differences in your maps instead of fighting for your position and your map. Once you embrace this idea, it creates space for you to expand. You allow more. You judge less. You observe instead of *fix*. You find more empathy. You find the capacity to remain curious, and you grow because you simply understand that the map is not the territory.

The Territory

The territory is exactly that. It's a completely objective, independent space that's up for debate. It's the detached, isolated space that is the focus of the conversation, not the actual conversation. The territory is the reality of something versus your perspective or representation of it. The territory is the actual person in the picture versus the picture itself. The territory is the world we all exist in, the world we are all experiencing through our own highly subjective maps. Know this: Everyone has a map and a story, both of which are being used to navigate the territory. Once you understand that space, the world gets so much clearer.

The heart of this book provides a breakdown of how to understand and heal your map. The first section is about awareness, knowing you can only change the things you are aware of. We'll dive into all the tools you need to heal your map, including a bit about NLP, what it is and how to use it, strategies and coaching models that are incredibly impactful and still user-friendly, the anchors and triggers that hold all those strategies together as well as the powerful stories we tell ourselves that make it all true. Lastly, I'll unveil how unprocessed trauma plays a role in creating your map and how to heal the remnants it leaves behind. The clarity that people find in this space is life changing.

Why Does the Map Matter?

What a great question! Your map matters because, although we are all sharing this collective territory, each one of us is experiencing something completely different. How can you and I find alignment in this common space when our perspectives are so different? The key to this is understanding that each of us is navigating the territory with our own map. The more clarity I find inside my own map, the more clarity I can find in the territory. The more clarity you find on your map, the more clarity you find in the territory. The more you can understand your own map, the better you can navigate. The more you understand the map you are creating for your children, the more of the territory they get to experience.

You see, your map matters because all the same ideas also apply to you. The more you understand about yourself, the more impactful you can be in the world. The more you know about how your map works, what affects it and how to edit it, the more unstoppable you become in the territory. Once you fully understand your map, the territory becomes your playground. The more you understand about your map, the more curious you become about others (maps).

The map matters because it's exactly what you are using to navigate through this amazing world, the territory. Think about all the different hats you wear in the world—not just in the present day, but all the different places you have been and all the different versions of yourself you have grown through. How powerful would it have been to have had access to your map back then? What could have been possible had you known then what you know now? Knowing that we cannot work backwards, imagine what's possible now, moving forward. How much more access will you have, and how much more impactful will you be once you understand the power of your map and where it can lead you?

The more you understand the map as a teacher, the more territory you can teach to your students.

The more you understand your map as a coach, the more you can teach the territory to the players.

The more you understand your map as a sister, the more you can share the territory with your siblings.

The more you understand your map as a spouse, the more you can share the territory with your partner.

The more you understand your map as a business owner, the more territory your clients and your employees get to experience.

The more you understand your map as a writer, the more context you can bring to your readers.

The more you understand your map as a friend, the more you can engage your friends.

Simply put, the more you understand, the more you can experience.

Remember back in very early elementary school when you learned how to write with that big fat pencil? Then they also gave you those chunky crayons to try and color with? Those were the fundamental tools you started with. As you progressed through school, you got smaller crayons, but there were only eight of them in the box. Then as you aged up, your box of crayons went from twenty-four to forty-eight and then to sixty-four and maybe even to 124 crayons. The boxes of 124 crayons even had a built-in pencil sharpener. The more colors you were given, the more creative you could be. In that same space, your pencil went from that big chunky pencil, to a thin one, and then to a pen, or maybe a fancy gel writer. If you were really lucky, you took a typing class and you learned how to type. And now, in the present day, you mostly communicate by typing.

Now imagine how different your ability to communicate would be if you were still stuck with that fat pencil today, trying to articulate every detail with this clearly outdated tool. How effective do you believe you could be? Your map is the same way. The more you understand your map the more access you have to yourself and all the territory around you. Odds are high you will have normalized that big, chunky pencil, and it's possible you might be watching others communicate effectively but not know how they make it look so easy.

Imagine what will be possible once you not only access and update your map but also start intentionally using it. How much better will your ability to communicate be with an updated map? How different will approaching conversations be with an awareness of others' maps and the role they play for them? How much different will your ability to perceive the territory be when you consciously know your map's role in it?

How magical would this world be if every single person on this planet understood not only that there *was* a map but understood their very own map? The more you understand your map, the easier it is to affect change.

As you start to consider these ideas, take a moment and reflect.

Questions for Insight

➢ What have you learned thus far?

➢ What's surfacing for you, and/or what are you learning about your map?

Chapter 2

How Maps Are Built

Starting at conception, your biggest influencers in building your map are your parent(s), or anyone acting in that capacity, and, if present, any medical professionals—doctors, dentists, pediatricians, ER staff, nurses, or surgeons. These influencers are your trusted voices. In your early formative years as a child, those trusted voices are also the ones who build your map. As you mature and gain more conscious awareness, you start developing discernment and start making your own decisions. Those decisions are based upon the depths of information and how much or how little information you have on your map.

A trusted voice is any voice that you believed as a child. Trust is the conduit of influence. During childhood, you believed the adults around you and absorbed information from the environments they allowed you to witness. Your brain was malleable in your younger years (and maybe still is), and you held guidance from your trusted voices in high regard. Your map collected everything—the good, the bad, the healthy things, the unhealthy things, and everything in between.

In those early years, most children have limited access to trusted voices aside from friends and family members until they reach school age. When my youngest daughter was four years old, she needed a trusted voice bigger than mine (her pediatrician) to remind her that she could not fly. My guess is she witnessed me being a driven athlete, who rarely, if ever, took no for an answer from my body, and then modeled that behavior. This much-needed information came in shortly after she jumped off a playscape and broke her humerus bone while attempting to fly. Kids listen to, adhere to and build their maps in alignment with what they witness and absorb in their environments and from the trusted voices that validate their observations.

When you reached school age, teachers and coaches were added to your list of trusted voices. Until early adulthood, those are the four trusted voices that have unknowingly been allowed to build your map: your parents, your teachers, your coaches and medical professionals. Your parents, caregivers and teachers have held the biggest voices and left the deepest imprints on your map. They were the trusted voices that you spent the most time with in those early, formative and impressionable years. And because you had such young, open minds, it's also these voices who have most deeply affected you.

You have taken the world in with them as your guide. They have held the light, lit the path and guided you through with *their* interpretations and *their* map, all the while unknowingly building *your* map. You placed all your trust in them and in the wisdom they handed down to you. You believed and trusted them and built your map in accordance with that guidance, both knowingly and unknowingly. You learned morals, values, rules, culture and all the things both spoken to you and modeled for you. This much-needed information created your individualized, incredibly subjective map.

All Maps Are Not Created Equal

Although everyone deserves the right to live the life they've always imagined, not everyone has a map that leads them to that destination. Know that regardless of who built your map, all maps are not created equal. Allow me to slow down and acknowledge a bit of information. It would be completely normal if you are reading this thinking, I trusted them because I had to, even when they were modeling things that felt out of alignment. You placed your trust in these relationships because it was the only option you had access to at that point in time, whether their concepts proved to be right or wrong.

From your firsthand experiences, it would also make complete sense if survival mode kicked in and helped you get through some of those tough moments, or possibly all of them. Survival mode kicked in to keep you safe and it simply took over. The earlier this moment occurred the more you have normalized the presence of the adrenaline and cortisol pumping through your physical being just to stay alive. In the areas where there were supposed to be trust and healthy role models, neither were available. Your fight or flight mode kept you moving. Although that pace, energy and feeling may have felt completely normal for you, please know it was incredibly dysfunctional. I say that with massive amounts of love and absolutely free from judgment. I'm simply creating awareness for you around that old, contracted energy and inviting you to release it when the time is right.

These relationships created your ability to trust, and they are the foundational spaces you still build upon today, whether they were healthy or not. If they were not healthy, remember that it was simply all you had access to. Without access to healthy role models, you are left to your own devices. You learn to tolerate. You learn to behave accordingly. You learn to hold it in. You learn to shut it down. And without access to your voice and your feelings, you learn to normalize the patterns. You have zero conscious awareness that there is another way. You also have minimal, if any, ability to build functional relationships on top of the dysfunctional foundation that was created for you.

Present-Day Mapping

Every time you hear words or re-experience things, they bounce off your previously built map and pull forward whatever meaning and response they were originally encoded in, even if that meaning is decades old, ineffective or unhealthy. Each moment of your life has been recorded on your map, and the meaning that you give to those moments was defined and recorded decades ago. That encoded response is simply all you know. I share this in hopes of creating some awareness around what you have normalized. If you were raised in a highly frenetic environment, your immediate response to things may be a dramatic, emergency pattern, laced with adrenaline. Yet if you were raised in a calm, emotionally regulated household, you may have more of a collected, intentional response, focused on the well-being of everyone present. The idea here is that your map was originally encoded in the level of intensity it still operates in today. The foundational space that it was created in has built your ability to, or not to, emotionally regulate yourself.

If your map was built in a juxtaposed space that left you unable to access or process your feelings, it's possible that you now have zero capacity to build emotionally regulated relationships. Those opportunities simply do not exist, and you have normalized the effects of that gaping wound. To take it a step further, if you have never felt your feelings, how do you teach your kids to feel? If you have never used your voice, how do you teach your kids to use their voices?

When something impacts you deep enough to leave a mark, know that it affected your map. That experience became anchored on your map and most likely unknowingly built an unconscious belief (more on anchors in chapter 10). Anchors and beliefs are built quickly and consistently over time. The more the same pattern of trauma occurs, the deeper the anchor sets, the more embedded the belief becomes and the more fluent you become in that level of energy.

Psychological Sunburn

When there is an open wound on your map, it's like a psychological sunburn. It's triggered by even the smallest pictures, words, or memories, and as soon as someone or something engages it, you instantaneously react. Your response is not flexible. It's not changeable. It's not justifiable. It's simply triggered and there's a response. The button has been pushed and you are back into the throws of heightened fight or flight. This is a prime example of unhealed memories that are anchored on your map. Your response to someone or something engaging this anchor is highly unconscious and most often comes without warning.

My goal with this book is to teach you that your response is actually independent of the other person yet is directly related to the previous memory it engaged. However, because the two are tied together, it makes sense that you would want to place blame. Know that the button was there long before said person engaged it. It's about the button that was engaged not the name that was spoke, the song that was played, the word that was said, it's about the memory and emotion it pulls forward today, not about the person engaging it. It feels exactly like a terrible sunburn. As soon as it's spoken, your neurology responds. You feel as if the world just smacked your blazing hot, red sunburn. That response is encoded into your map. That response has been evolving and intensifying over time. That response can also be edited. That memory can be released. The button can be dismantled and will dissipate. The only thing required for this is your conscious, intentional choice.

All Maps Are Editable

Learning how to access the highest parts of yourself, on demand, is a huge part of self-mastery. Most people are navigating around this planet with an incredibly outdated paper map but are expecting the results of a modern-day GPS map. Take a moment and reflect on the last time your phone alerted you that it needed to be updated. As annoying as the updates are, and as risky as they may feel, they are imperative to your phone functioning properly. Your map is much the same.

My guess is that at least two or three times a year, maybe more, your phone makes such requests. Knowing what you know now about your map, how many times has your map been updated? Odds are high the answer is never. Knowing that, how old are some of the beliefs and patterns that your map has built for you? Is it possible that your outdated map might be the reason you keep getting off track and are unable to accomplish your ideal outcome? Your map is the tool that you use to navigate the world every day, yet it's never been updated. Odds are also incredibly high there are some deeply embedded beliefs on your map. Most of them emanate from fourth grade or younger. In those fourth-grade days, in the depths of elementary school, you were ten years old at best. My question is where else in your life you are allowing a ten-year-old to make decisions for you.

I share that in hopes of creating awareness around the idea that your behaviors come as a result of the roots and the story that they're founded in. Until you understand that story, it's impossible to change your behavior or your outcome. For me personally, I was raised in an incredibly frenetic environment and was extremely traumatized as a child, not so much in my own home but absolutely at school and in my social world. I was not even aware that calm was an option as it was never modeled to me. I normalized that story. I normalized that pace. I normalized survival mode.

My energy and my story created an outcome I didn't align with, and every day it felt like I was swimming upstream. It wasn't until I learned NLP and learned about my map, my roots, my energy and my old, incredibly normalized story that my life began to change. I had to gain awareness of my internal map. This book is the story of that journey and all the tools I used to get there. Gaining awareness of your internal map and then learning the skills it takes to edit it has to happen before anything externally can follow. HARD STOP.

Allow me to pause and highlight something incredibly important before we move forward. This content is not against your parents or against the teachers and people that have helped create your map. This is more about the idea that you were guided by your trusted voices, and they led you with the only map they had access to—theirs. Odds are high, as you begin to explore your map, you will find things that will challenge you, and you may want to place blame, shame or anger. Know that this is normal. Also know that everyone in life is doing the best they can with the tools they have access to now or had access to in that time and space. I am certain that my own parents know more now than they did when they were raising me and my siblings—much the same as I do now, as a parent of two kids myself. Leaning into Maya's concept, know that the unhealthy content that you are housing on your map was not placed there with intent. It was simply the act of people not knowing any better. This book is about learning, knowing, and doing better from this point forward.

Moving forward, this is about the map and the story that you have unknowingly created from that journey. The more awareness you have around those two things, the more intentional you can be about your life today. As you grow, oftentimes you either get stuck in an old version of yourself or have a knee-jerk reaction to place blame on someone else for your current reality. Remember that pattern serves no one. The goal is instead to learn to build a new pattern.

Create awareness around today.

Understand how to move forward.

Build an intentional tomorrow.

Once you understand your map, you start to communicate better, and you make better connections. You start finding more patience with other people because you realize that much like your map, other people are simply just a reflection of their map.

The Roots of Trauma

As you grow, acknowledging the impact and power that trauma may have held on to your map is imperative. I realize that trauma can be a triggering word. Let's stop for a moment and seek to understand what trauma is and why it's so powerful. Trauma is the emotional and physiological response you experience to a deeply disturbing event. Trauma is truly anything that takes you out of a coherent state and into a fight or flight response. Regardless of how big or small the event was or how often it occurred, it was recorded on your map and it created an anchor. The more often it happened, the more you normalized it. One thing I know for sure is the more heightened an emotion, the deeper the anchor is embedded onto your map. Trauma is all around you and you have heavily normalized the impact it has created on you, your family and society as a whole.

Each one of us has experienced trauma. It's an inevitable part of our lives. Learning to process trauma and/or learning healthy coping skills is an essential part of life. Building resilience can be a powerful tool yet processing the trauma is still necessary. In reality, most people simply normalize the pain, internalize the effects it had on them and keep moving forward. The question becomes how much trauma one human can handle, or how much trauma are you normalizing and allowing in simply because you do not know any better.

Finding a Mask

Coming from a person who was consistently traumatized as a child, I now know that I hid behind my humor. I masked my pain with humor. Humor was the largest form of protection that I could access. The compound effects of my consistent trauma embedded ideas into my map like: I am not a good student. I am not as smart as my siblings. Bullying is normal. I am too tall. I am too big. I am too independent. I am way too distracted, yet if I can make them laugh, it deflects the uncomfortable energy. Looking back, I was trying to pay attention and trying to find my center, yet my nervous system was stuck in fight or flight, way too busy trying to stay alive. It was too much for one tiny system to handle. Due to that overload, my nervous system normalized the fight or flight response too. And because I was always on guard, I was also always distracted.

I normalized survival mode. I normalized it because being off guard hurt more than being ready. If I allowed myself to relax, it created more nervous energy than staying on guard. It also left me open for attack. Staying on guard, with the adrenaline and cortisol pumping, kept me safe. Being on guard also removed me from being great at lots of things. In those days, it was often noted that I was not nearly as great as my siblings were at things like climbing trees, school sports and even burning calories. Looking back, my mind and body were more focused on keeping me safe. My physiology was busy. Overloaded. Distracted. Consumed. And the aftermath that those effects created for me meant that I barely graduated from high school—yet I was funny AF. That's what carried me—humor.

My childhood was spent, on and off, with me struggling as a student. It took me being an extremely uneducated teen mom and having my first daughter before I even thought about school or the role it played in life. Two years into college and having failed multiple classes, with a five-year-old in tow, it was then that they discovered I only had a sixth-grade education. It's no wonder I wasn't as great as my siblings were.

My physiology and my neurology were consumed elsewhere, creating a huge educational deficit masked by humor. What had been anchored on my map was "I'm not smart" so why would I even waste my time trying to pay attention or learn if I'm not smart? With that outlook, my map allowed me to get out of assignments with humor. It distracted my parents, who thought she's not very smart, *but* she's super funny. And although it shielded me from the pain, the Band-Aid I created with humor never actually healed the wound. It simply masked the symptoms.

Awareness Equals Access

The most powerful thing we can learn here is pure and utter awareness. This is not about right and wrong, it's simply about awareness. Awareness equals access. You don't know what you don't know, and you can only change the things you are aware of. Awareness allows you the space to self-discover your own map. This self-discovery creates freedom for you to intentionally access your patterns, which allows you to make effective, sustainable edits to your map. Those edits create the capacity for new decisions, which lead you to your ideal outcome.

Everyone wants to live the life they have imagined, yet most people are not sure how to create or find permanent access to that space. As a mastery-level coach and licensed NLP trainer, the most powerful thing I can offer you is awareness—awareness around how you got where you are today and where you can go from here. The more you know, the more you can change. Each of us has our own journey. You can grow, you can learn and you can heal through it, once you have an intentional, updated map.

Humor Only Carries You So Far

With an incredible amount of help and tons of guidance, I went on to finish my associate degree, an accomplishment nine years in the making. I then completely shocked the world, myself included, and finished undergrad and graduate school, both with honors. Me, the uneducated, funny kid who barely graduated from high school. What occurred over that time-span was that as my awareness grew, it created more and more access—access to myself, access to what I now know as my map, access to my patterns, my beliefs and my stories—which allowed me the time and space to heal. As I healed, I grew. And as both occurred, I started to understand and release the trauma.

What I know now is that what set me apart from my siblings as a learner was the internal environments we had created over time. Our roof was the same. Our maps were different. I was contracted in trauma, unable to access the expanded states necessary for learning. Their default space was expanded, allowing them to explore the territory in a much different way (more on expanded and contracted states in chapter 8).

States of Consciousness

I started studying NLP with a side of Esther Hicks. Both of those studies became an integral part of my map (more on both later). Through coaches training, multiple NLP trainings, Abraham Hicks seminars, trauma courses and a multitude of other studies, I began to tear apart and rebuild my map. I became super fluent in what I valued. I started to build boundaries (that's an entire book of its own). And the more I healed, the more I unmasked, and the more I found the parts of me that were deeply buried in old, paralyzing childhood trauma.

From that space, I transformed. I edited my map. I released the parts of my old story that no longer served me. I healed the lingering, unprocessed bits of trauma that were woven into my fabric. With time, I eventually became this highly intentional, connected version of Jodee, consciously using my story as leverage. Without my story and my past, I wouldn't have this much access to myself nor be as impactful as a coach. Learning to step outside of my story allowed me to start healing the roots that created my old, unconscious world. Coaching others through that same healing journey is now my life's work.

Understand what's possible: you can honor your old story and release it at the same time.

Questions for Insight

> Knowing what you know now, what are the things you believe you have normalized over time that no longer serve you?

_____

_____

_____

_____

_____

➢ How old were you when that pattern was created?
If multiple patterns come up for you, please notate
and date each one.

➢ What stands out for you about your map and the
access it has created for you?

➢ What does your map currently prevent you from
doing or accessing?

➢ What story has your map created for you?

➢ What does that story prevent you from
doing or being?

Chapter 3

Your Map, Your Story

The Future Is Ahead of You

The foundations of human behavior begin with each person's map. The phrase the map is not the territory embraces the idea that you are not your past. Your past is simply a piece to your story; it's not your whole story. It's simply what's happened thus far. I am here to tell you that you can leave it right where it was and move forward once you become aware of the hold it has on you. Living in the past serves no one.

The more you understand about your map, the more you will understand not only about yourself but also about the people around you. Understanding how your map was created leads you directly to your habits, your beliefs, and your outcomes. Once you understand that process for yourself, it becomes easier to understand it and teach it to others. It also creates more conscious leaders, parents, coaches, and educators. Although I am a newly emerging expert, one thing I know for sure is the more fluent and conscious you become of your own behaviors, the more you can intentionally and consciously impact the world. Reliving what happened yesterday is completely unnecessary. Your future is ahead of you.

As you move forward, embrace the idea that the way other people feel about your journey, does not impact your reality unless you let it. Their opinions are simply a reflection of their map, not yours. Their words are about them, and the words that people say to you are not true until you make them true. Oftentimes your old story might believe the words someone is sharing, while your new story is perplexed by who would ever believe such a thing. Honor your new story and embrace the idea that everyone is navigating around this beautiful territory with their very own, very subjective, personalized map.

The words that people say to you are not true until you make them true.

Editing Your Map

The more you understand about your map and all the incredible things it houses, the more you can be an intentional map maker for yourself, your kids and the people you surround yourself with. Now that you know this information, your map is your responsibility. The information provided in this book will give you direct access to your own map, your values, your beliefs, your patterns and everything else you will need to edit your map. This information will create incredible awareness for you and allow you to better understand your trusted voices and the roles you play with your own trusted voice.

What's currently missing from the very much normalized and current Western approach to mental health is the understanding that normalizing the effects of trauma and medicating the symptoms it creates is not a sustainable solution (more on both later). Expanding on that idea, if you were born into a family of addicts, whether the vice is drugs, alcohol, food, gambling, shopping or whatever it is, odds are high that you do not have access to healthy coping skills. Your vice of choice replaces your ability to cope and self-regulate. Your vice fills the gap where your coping skills should exist. Expecting you to have the healthy capacity to cope is beyond ludicrous, as those skills are not part of your map nor are they accessible to you. There is a gap where those skills should be, and it's filled with your vice of choice. Due to that compound effect, filling the gap, ending the feeling and numbing the pain unconsciously becomes your number one goal.

Normalizing Your Vice

Odds are high that if healthy, functional coping skills were not taught or modeled to you in your home, then they are not something you can lean into and utilize. They are not something you have consistent access to, if access exists at all. Using a vice to normalize that gap is simply ordinary life for you. Creating awareness around that gap and the vice you use as a filler is an integral step in learning to heal. Before you can take action and create the desire to change, you must first be aware that the gap exists. Even when the gap is acknowledged, you can still only use the tools you have access to, or the ones that *feel* normal to you.

In that same space, you often unknowingly seek out drama because that's the only language your nervous system is fluent in. You seek out heavy conversations, or run away from them, in a response to what feels familiar. We are creatures of habit and are drawn toward familiar things. We make friends, take jobs, join communities and create relationships in the vibrations that feel familiar.

If you're curious where your default energy lies, pause for a moment, pick up your phone and jot down a few lists.

➤ Who were the last five people you spoke to?

➤ What were the last five posts you engaged with on social media?

➤ What was the general energy behind the last five text messages you sent?

➤ What were the last five songs you listened to?

➤ What were the last five shows you have watched on TV (or on your phone)?

➤ What was the energy behind the last five emails you sent?

My guess is you are getting the idea. The things you fill your life with are the things that feel familiar to you (more on this in chapter 9).

Understand this, much like your childhood, the world you create around kids, consciously or unconsciously, becomes the world they grow up in. It becomes what they normalize. The conversations you have and those you negate; the emotions you allow and the ones you shove down; the words you use to describe yourself and the stories you build around what happens are the exact things kids will normalize.

All things either grow you or limit you. They either make you expand, or they make you contract (more on both in chapter 8). Understanding the difference and gaining conscious awareness of how both work is imperative for sustainable growth. I started life off as an extremely uneducated teen mom. The story I kept telling myself was that I was going to figure it out. The stories people told around me were that my life was over, and I had ruined it by becoming a mom so early. The limitations people place around you are a direct reflection of their map and how they feel about themselves; they are not about you. Read that sentence again. Had I listened to the advice-givers in those days I'd probably still be living in my hometown, making minimum wage, still making terrible, unhealthy decisions, and justifying it by saying but they said I can't.

The Weight of Shame

When you stay committed to your unknown, unhealthy map, it leaves evidence in its wake. Take for example the power of shame. When you shame a child from the lowest level of energy, there is no response that the child can give that satisfies you. The shame is about your map. The shame is not about the child or the child's map. It's about the way you have been taught to process information. The shame you may project is deeply imprinting a space on the child's map. It's adding content to the child's map that shame is the answer to undesired behavior. There is no learning opportunity present for the child, just a heavy burden of carrying the unhealed shame, further teaching the child that when they don't achieve your ideal outcome, shame is the result.

Understanding the weight of the shame loop being imprinted into that child, and the historical response it will forever create, is beyond powerful. The loop of shame just gets recycled. The shame is passed from the adult to you as a child.

Then you grow into the adult who uses it on your children, and the cycle repeats. Gaining awareness and removing things like this from your map simply creates better humans. Imagine how many other unknown, unhealthy behavior loops are currently cycling on your map.

Instead of feeling hurt, offended, wronged or judged, think about what it would feel like to believe the response you needed at that moment, whether you were the adult or the child, was just not part of the responder's map. There was a gap between your needs and their map. Becoming aware of your map and the role it plays, not only in your life but also in the lives of people around you is how you affect change. Becoming conscious, slowing down, and embracing the idea that you are constantly using your map and affecting the maps of others is the key. Again, the words that people say to you are not true until you make them true. With every fiber of my being, I understand human behavior at the deepest levels. You are the product of the culture and environment you grow up in, yet that does not have to be your final destination.

Your Childhood Mirror

Much like the concept that water self-levels, we seek out and are attracted to similar energies, similar maps and similar vibes to level us out. We unconsciously seek out spaces similar to those that built us, even when they're highly dysfunctional or unhealthy. We have normalized the presence and feelings that come with them. We are unconsciously fluent in dysfunction. This is also precisely why people's words affect us so much. We know their opinions or thoughts are not in alignment with who we're becoming, yet the energy behind them feels so familiar. Editing your map will require your consistent awareness of that juxtaposed energy.

What determines the way you show up in the world today is the way you remember your childhood and the impact you currently allow your childhood to have on your natural-born talent. The story you created around that space and around what's possible from the summation of it brings you to the present day. What keeps you apart from your goals is your consistent and normalized reflection of that childhood trauma. I get deep into the trenches of trauma in this book. Regardless of whether you've had one major trauma, several major traumas, or a million little microtraumas, they all had the capacity to wound you and leave a scar.

Content runs deep inside everyone's map. All the energy behind those unhealed remarks, events, memories, feelings, thoughts and challenges are only so easily triggered because they're still present on your map. The resistance they create has been so normalized and embedded into your everyday life that you have little conscious awareness of them. Removing them from your map is the goal. Healing those spaces is my fluent language and my life's work. Maps are the main tool used to navigate the territory. When maps are left untreated, the remnants of those unhealed traumatic events will, over time, create emotional dysregulation or arrested emotional development.

I have spent the past three decades digging through my own map as well as extensively, formally educating myself. The culmination of my formal education, my life experience and my integrated, layer-by-layer, evidence-based, holistic approach to mental wellness, has created my well-rounded approach to treating and removing root causes. Once I learned NLP, the roots became my main focus. I believe my approach is beyond accurate. Learning how to stop medicating symptoms and start addressing root causes first starts with understanding the map.

I've been a part of and have witnessed numerous Western modalities, attempting to medicate these spaces and change the behavior or outcome, yet they never investigate the roots and anchors that birthed them. Teaching you about your map, the power of intention, neuro linguistic programming, conscious choice, and the law of vibration is my intention. With that info, I truly believe you will have the power to unlock all the things that feel stuck, release old stories that no longer serve you, heal the wounds that are often triggered by others' words and begin building the life you want, intentionally and with great purpose.

You cannot force nature . . . only nurture.

—JEWEL[2]

Now that you know what you know, imagine how impactful your map has been in your life.

The brilliant Alan Watts once shared that human behavior is much like embroidering: the final piece that everyone sees is nearly impeccable, yet when you flip it over, the back is a total mess. You are much like these pieces of embroidery. You share your beautiful exterior with everyone around you while intentionally hiding the total mess of an interior. You hide as if you are afraid of judgment because all you can see from your perspective is everyone else's beautiful, impeccable exterior.

Vulnerability only weighs on you when you're trying to hide it from the world.

Yet how often do you stop to realize that in order for others to have such a beautiful exterior, there must be a messy interior somewhere too? There's a yin to every yang.[3]

My guess is that you are beginning to discover and uncover things about your map that might challenge your thinking. It might excite you to know that your map is not your *fault*, or that your map is in fact editable. It may also make you uncomfortable, maybe even a bit ashamed. It might make you sad. It may provoke you. Or maybe you already know some of this content, and you're just here to learn how to edit your map. Know that this is all normal. You did not arrive where you are today by planning every piece of your journey. You've landed here because this is where your map guided you to land. This is where it has navigated you. It's more of a collective default.

Hiding yourself from the world is a natural reaction, especially when we have some awareness that there may be judgment. Judgment is harsh. It hurts. It can reach even the deepest parts of us that remain unhealed, further solidifying our negative self-talk. Judgment can be paralyzing. Embrace the idea that you've done an amazing job navigating with the map you were given. With this book, you can learn how to edit the areas that feel stuck, immoveable or obstructive to your success. With deep consistent work, everything on your map is editable. The best thing about this is you are only a product of your environment if you continue to live inside the container that it has built around you. HARD STOP. Go ahead and read that again. I'll wait.

Product of Your Environment

You are only a product of your environment if you continue to knowingly remain in the space it has created around you even though it no longer fits you or your goals. Release yourself from that space. Release your childhood from your adulthood. Take a moment and reflect on the present day. Is your childhood hijacking or dictating your adulthood, or is your adulthood managing your childhood?

Take a moment if you need it. Jot down what's coming up for you.

It's common to believe things like *this is just who I am.* Instead try taking a moment to acknowledge a more accurate statement like:

— this is who I have unconsciously become over time;

— this is the only version of me that I have access to at this moment;

— this is all I am allowing myself to be right now; or maybe even

— this is all I'm comfortable accessing.

Know that although all those responses are completely normal. You are so much more than you can ever dream to be. Gaining this level of self-awareness begins to bridge the gap between who you currently are and who you are capable of becoming. It's about creating awareness around the map you are using and where it's currently leading you. You heard my story. You know where I came from. The more aware I became of my story and the patterns those stories created for me, the more I began to lead with intention and things began to change. It was all about awareness. The more awareness I had, the more intention I created to make the changes necessary. This is not about fixing; it's about finding enough awareness to create the level of access you need to change. The more awareness you have, the more you can unpack. The more you unpack your story, the more you will start to uncover your patterns. The more self-aware you become, the more access you have to you.

Repetition Creates Normalization

The more you repeat a pattern, the deeper the groove it embeds into your brain. Over time, these deeply patterned grooves become your normal, default behavior. The deeper the grooves, the more neuroplasticity you build around them. And in a very short period, your responses run at a highly unconscious level, needing very little, if any, input from you. Overtime and with great repetition, they create a loop of their own and simply run on auto-play, validating the notion *this is just who I am* without any conscious or intentional desire. The more often you run a pattern (using your neural pathways), the deeper the groove becomes and the more embedded it is into your physiology. It becomes your normalized, default response. As Dr. Joe Dispenza shares, brain cells that fire to-gether, wire together.[4]

Allow me to pause. I know neuroplasticity may sound like a huge term, yet it's a very simple process. Neuroplasticity is simply your brain's ability to assimilate and adjust to new habits, either by creating new ones or by releasing old ones. Because your brain is constantly working toward efficiency, it creates patterns as shortcuts to simplify repetitive tasks. Much like your childhood bike path, the more you use the pathways, the easier it is to effortlessly find and use the path. The more you use the path, the more embedded it becomes and the less conscious you are of its presence. Eventually, you run the pattern with zero conscious effort on a continuous loop. The challenging thing about neuroplasticity is attempting to interrupt and change an unconscious, embedded pattern, especially if it is running on a loop.

You see, you, me and every other human being on this planet all operate in patterns. We behave in patterns. We work in patterns. We play in patterns. We love in patterns. And we hide in patterns. We do everything in patterns. The more we run a pattern, or series of patterns, the more they loop together. Over time, the looped responses run on default. Understanding patterns and loops are foundational to understanding how human behavior works.

Although interrupting the patterns that no longer serve you is the key to sustainable change, attempting to change directions while using the same path, pattern or loop is often easier than it sounds. Once you create awareness around the path and the looped response, you can consciously choose not to use it. At that point, the more overgrown it becomes and the more awkward it feels to use it. Creating conscious awareness of all the different pieces of the loop (the path) helps open more windows of opportunity to stop the loop from closing. The more awareness you have, the more success you will find.

That was a lot, so let's take a moment to recap. Neuroplasticity is the art of embedded response grooves and encompasses the idea that the more times you repeat a task, the more you unknowingly embody the pattern. Eventually, the pattern runs effortlessly with zero conscious awareness and becomes your normalized, default space. This is how patterns are created. The patterns only change with age-appropriate, intentional, conscious effort and guidance.

We all make multiple patterns for many things. We have linguistic patterns, behavioral patterns, emotional patterns and neurological patterns, all of which work with minimal guidance and input. Many of these patterns run unconsciously and were created and normalized well before you hit elementary school.

And although they are all working in concert towards efficiency, they're not always healthy, productive, nor functional.

Trust Is the Conduit of Influence

I share this with full disclosure. You trusted your parents, your caregivers and the trusted voices who supported you as a small child as they taught you all the things you know and use today. My question is how conscious were you of how healthy, or unhealthy, the information you absorbed was. Knowing that these are the people who created your map, without your knowledge or your consent, how accurate and healthy was the content you collectively built your map with? Remember from chapter 2 that this is not about placing blame or creating conflict, it's simply about gaining awareness. Without awareness, you are left to unknowingly repeat their generationally learned cycle.

It's much like entrainment. Entrainment is the idea that you move inside the cadence of the environment you were built in. Like dancers who find their cadence in music. Writers find their cadence in words. Teachers find their cadence in the classrooms they build. You are much the same. Your collective vibration was born from the environment that built you. You have been trained to respond to the cues that were placed on your map, even the unhealthy ones. If that cadence is not creating the outcome you are looking for, interrupt the pattern. Pick up the needle. Stop the music.

You see, some of our maps were created with broken pencils. The more awareness you have around those spaces, the more access you will gain of yourself. Although no one would intentionally create another's map with a broken pencil, you can only use the tools you have access to. In that moment in time, the only access your mapmaker had was what they used. And by default, their tools now become your tools, regardless of their ability to accomplish the task at hand.

Toddler Tantrums

Think about a toddler's perspective. They instinctively know how to work a room. If they need something, they ask, whine or cry until their need is met. They also know how to gain a reward from their parental figure, or whoever it needs to be. Whether it's a sucker, a cookie or even a parent's full attention, they know how to get to that end result. They have mastered this behavioral pattern in just a few short years. They have used a trial-and-error approach and have been compiling information to get to the reward. They ask, beg or throw a gigantic, full-on, dramatic toddler tantrum. This learned be-havior is a temporary space. It was created to be used for survival. It was also created in place of the toddler's inability to use words, as they are just learning to speak. A toddler's inability to articulate and understand leads them to use what they know, which is brute force, tears or both.

Much like that toddler, once you learn words, learn how to communicate and learn how to manage your emotions, you start to communicate by using your voice and verbalizing your needs versus throwing a tantrum. The challenge comes in when you allow that toddler pattern to become the only way you communicate and function, instead of as the transitional space of growth and learning that it was designed to be. We'll learn more about emotional regulation and conscious map editing later.

Understand How You Communicate

Your brain is wired for two things, efficiency and belonging. You are always working toward or against one of those two things. The environment that you were created in becomes the language that you communicate with. Gaining awareness around how that impacts your movement today is how you create change. Staying in the patterns and grooves, expecting a different outcome is not possible. Or if it is temporarily possible, it's definitely not sustainable nor will it lead to the lasting change you are seeking. Using childlike tactics does not create adult responses in much the same way that treating the symptoms does not change the root problem.

When your body has a symptom, treating only the symptom does not change the root cause that created the symptom. It simply and temporarily soothes the pain, but there's no way of knowing if or when it will return. For example, if you are driving down the freeway and your check engine light comes on, what is your response? Do you just unplug the light and hope the car keeps going? Or do you call a mechanic and allow him to get under the hood and find the source of the problem? The light is a notification that there's a problem; it's not the actual problem. It's simply a light that alerts you that there's a problem inside. Sustainable change is not about embracing *what's wrong*, it's more about being curious about what pattern is running that continues to produce this consistent outcome.

Changing the outcome of a normalized pattern, by treating symptoms, does not create lasting change unless you identify the pattern and find the root cause that the symptom is emanating from. Unplugging the check engine light does make the light go off, yet there's no telling how long that solution will last. Sustainable change requires a new, intentional pattern. Have you been conditioned to run around with your engine light on expecting stellar results, hoping that its presence does not impact your ideal outcome? Or do you pause and take care of yourself? Hopefully, you're picking up on the idea that medicating the symptom does not change the root, it only temporarily soothes the current result.

In order to achieve the outcome you desire, you must first understand the pattern that creates it. Understanding and implementing patterns of success on purpose is achieved by learning about your map and spending more time mastering success patterns and less time trying to temporarily soothe the symptoms created by old patterns. A successful pattern will, by default, produce the sustainable outcome you desire.

The most powerful piece of this whole conversation is that when you are in these spaces you are *not* aware of it because you don't know what you don't know. You have normalized your responses and the emotions you have around them. Because of this, you may not recognize a dysfunctional pattern on your map. You may not realize a juxtaposed position that creates inconsistent results because it was created by your childhood programming or unprocessed childhood trauma, and it's simply a normal space for you. You may not realize that something triggers your emotions because it's so deeply rooted in who you are, and you have normalized that response. You may not realize that you have a childlike response to certain triggers because it's the only response you have and that's how you've always responded. This is a prime example of emotional dysregulation.

Emotional dysregulation, said best by Laurence Heller, develops when we are unable to feel our emotions, when they overwhelm us, or when they remain unresolved, when we are unable to manage powerful or difficult emotions, or when we are anxious or depressed, we are in a state of dysregulation.[5] Pushing your feelings down, not acknowledging them, and allowing them to build up only exacerbates the problem. These are the spaces where fear piles up. These are the spaces where anxiety grows. These are the spaces where addictions and mental illness sprout roots. These are the spaces that emotional dysregulation emanates from.

Emotional dysregulation leads to obsessions, compulsions, addictions, eating disorders, phobias, anxiety disorders, anger problems, learning disorders, personality disorders, inability to attach, affect regulations and a myriad of other things. These responses are created in attempts to regulate our systems. They are done in an attempt to establish connection and belonging. And overtime, these ineffective, unhealthy, destructive patterns become normalized. Understanding what it is that causes you to break your state is where your power lies. Medicating any of these areas is simply medicating a symptom. Understanding their roots is imperative.

Awareness is the biggest game changer in this whole theory. Awareness around these spaces creates the access necessary for change. Awareness leads to self-actualization. Without awareness, we are left to navigate the world with the only map we have access to. Left untreated, this is the perfect recipe for arrested development (more on arrested development in chapter 13).

When you live in and normalize emotional dysregulation, and you normalize consistently seeking *something* to make it stop, what you are really doing is seeking an external solution to *fix* the internal feelings. Once you understand this concept, and you understand your patterns inside it, it's then that you have the tools to change, to evolve and to become that next version of yourself. You must first understand that your internal programming must change before your external response will even move. Until that time comes, you will continue to believe that external things create your internal response. Nothing could be further from the truth. How beautiful will it be to find out who you really are versus who you've been programmed to be? Where can your new map take you?

Questions for Insight

> ➢ Looking at the groups of five things you wrote down earlier, what is the story behind their common energy?

> ➢ What stands out for you from your childhood and/ or current relationships that feeds that story?

➢ Does your map soothe who you used to be, or does it serve who you're becoming? If it soothes, what old story is it soothing?

_____

_____

_____

_____

➢ If you could build a new map and/or edit your current map, what changes would you make?

_____

_____

_____

_____

➢ What do you believe is missing from your map?

_____

_____

_____

_____

➤ How do you know that it's missing?

_____

_____

_____

_____

➤ What will your newly created map allow you to do, create or be?

_____

_____

_____

_____

_____

➤ What will it eliminate for you?

_____

_____

_____

_____

_____

Chapter 4

You Can Edit Your Map

It's always interesting to see how much pain and baggage people unknowingly carry around with them from their childhood and then later unintentionally pass on to their own children. The only way to interrupt that generational cycle is to understand and intentionally heal your map. If this content feels relevant to you, odds are high that you were raised in an environment with either an over-functioning parent or an under-functioning one. The over-functioning parent shielded you from the things that would hurt in the process of learning yet were the exact things that would grow you. The under-functioning parent likely did not have access to their own feelings, so they taught you innately to follow suit and ignore your feelings and push through. Both spaces unknowingly left you without the skills necessary to emotionally mature.

The pain that grows from those spaces over time is not the result of the first time you experienced the pain, but rather a result of the symptoms you continually experienced from the rooted, unprocessed trauma and the beliefs, stories and destruction it left behind. When you learn outside of a normal, well-adjusted, emotionally regulated role model, you are left to your own devices and learn to navigate the world with the map you were handed. Building conscious awareness around those patterns now is the goal. Reliving those moments is not necessary yet understanding the roots they created and then removing them from your map is.

The Compound Effect

Pain grows from the compounding of symptoms, not from the root problem. David Berger once shared that "if you can feel it, you can heal it," which further led to the idea that if you can talk about it, you can understand it. His words once again create awareness that this is not a permanent space. Regardless of how big or small the symptoms are that keep popping up for you, the key is to understand where the root source is and learn how to remove it, eradicating any further growth or pain from that source.[6]

Take a moment and jot down what's coming up for you.

> How old are some of the memories and/or patterns that come to mind?

_____

_____

_____

_____

_____

➢ When was the first time you remember running those patterns?

_____

_____

➢ What was the strongest emotion in the moment when that pattern was built?

_____

_____

➢ Who else was present the first time you ran it?

_____

_____

➢ What was the root cause of that first pattern?

_____

_____

➢ What is the story you have created from that pattern that is still running today? What are you making that mean today?

_____

_____

The Functions of a Parent

An over-functioning parent (OFP) hinders your ability to grow through life's challenges, leaving you with the inability to find healthy access to your emotions. Odds are high they too were raised by a similar parent or are parenting this way as a direct opposite response to how they were parented. Their inability to vocalize their needs left you in somewhat of a victim position. You find yourself constantly waiting for someone to come rescue, help or save you in certain situations, or you are simply unable to voice your needs. We'll dig deeper into OFP in chapter 9, referenced as Scissor Syndrome.

The under-functioning parent (UFP) is the complete opposite. These are the parental figures who dismiss your pain, dismiss your needs, and appear utterly oblivious to your deepest yearnings for connection. UFPs are fighters. They're willing to use their voice in an aggressive manner or are always willing to fight city hall yet are unable to find their softer side that allows connection, trust and intimacy with those they are closest to. This lack of emotional connection leaves you feeling empty, disconnected and almost invisible.

The most frustrating yet validating part of this concept is that people can only meet your needs to the capacity that they've met their own. They can only meet you as deeply as they've met themselves. Pause and read that as many times as needed until it's embedded in your being. People can only meet you to the capacity that they are willing to meet themselves. They can only recognize your pain to the extent that they have acknowledged their own pain. They can only hear your voice to the extent that they can hear their own. They can only validate your emotions to the capacity that they have validated their own. They can only value you to the extent that they value themselves. The depth of your map has been determined by the challenges, both healthy and unhealthy, you have experienced and normalized. And the depth of those challenges has, as a result, created incredibly different recollections that vary from person to person, dependent upon the impact it had on each person. This leads back to the fact that we can only observe things to the capacity that we observe ourselves.

Snorkeling versus Scuba Diving

Imagine the difference in stories that will be told from a snorkeler versus a scuba diver. Although they're both swimming in the same ocean, they have two completely different views. One is deep in the ocean, getting face-to-face and intimate with all aspects of deep-sea life, while the other is satisfied with a surface-level view. Same ocean. Two completely different perspectives. And although they're both swimming in the same waters, the answers they supply will reflect how deeply they have embraced the ocean.

People are the same. They can only experience you to the capacity that they have experienced themselves. They can only experience you through their own map. People understand you through the filter that their map creates. When you speak to other people, your words are filtered through their map. The meaning they create from what has been filtered is often different from what you thought you conveyed. Maps are filters.

When two people communicate, there are two maps involved and the territory. This is how things get easily misconstrued. When I speak to you, the content is filtered through my map, then through the territory, and then filtered again through your map as you create an understanding of it. When you respond back to me, you filter through your map, then through the territory, then I filter that through my map, creating my understanding. Having awareness of that process is what enables our ability to communicate effectively. I do not have access to your map' nor do you have access to mine. The easiest and most effective way we can communicate is to stay curious and ask questions for clarity.

Lost in Translation

This idea explains why so many things get lost in translation. It also supports the idea of how you may often feel misaligned with others because they tell you one thing and yet you interpret another. They may say *I love you*, yet their actions feel really outside of your version of love. A parent may say *no, you cannot have it* or *no, I'm not buying that* only to turn around and supply it. You may share with a partner *no, I don't want to do that*, yet they insist. A friend may say *I'll be there for you*, yet you feel as if you are constantly going it alone. These events leave you with an amazingly juxtaposed picture. How that gets translated onto your map may create beliefs for you like *people don't mean what they say* or *no doesn't mean no* or *my voice doesn't matter anyway.*

Your parent(s) may have shushed you as a child yet now become angry when you don't use your voice to speak up. There are also people who say things like *you should [fill in the blank]*. Know that the *you should* statement occurs when someone is attempting to overlap their map onto your situation. They make the ridiculous assumption that their guidance is helpful, yet it leaves you even more confused because you do not have access to their map,—or their *shoulds*. You literally don't know what they mean because they're teaching you from their map instead of getting curious about yours.

All these conflicting messages are encoded onto your map and create your navigational system. The more you understand them, the more access you will gain to change them. Dismantling some of these patterns may lead to your ability to find joy in the pain. Life's really not that challenging once you learn how to edit your map and stop swimming upstream. We normalize stress like it's a badge of honor yet rarely stop to recognize what's creating most of it. The only way to interrupt generational trauma is to repair your current map.

You are worth protecting.

You are worth investing in.

Your feelings are worthy of being validated.

Feel All the Feels

Feelings were given to you for a reason. Feelings are teachers, not permanent conditions. Feelings are an internal response to an external trigger. You are only capable of responding to these external triggers with the access you have been given on your map. I know it sounds crazy but stay with me. If somebody puts a bike in front of you and you don't know how to ride it, then you don't know how to use the bike. Once you learn how to ride, you're pretty unstoppable. You might fall a couple of times. You might skin your knee. You might feel pain, but before you know it you are off and riding. You are a confident rider and drift off into your own little world. Your mind works the same way. Once you know how to use it, you are unstoppable.

Using the bike analogy, how many times did you have to ride your bike before you had access to that confidence? How many times did you have to ride before you were comfortable riding with one hand? Learning the bike takes time, and it's not something someone else can teach you. You must actually trust yourself and get on the bike and ride. No one taught you how to ride this bike of emotions. It's ok to not know. It will take time to learn where the patterns are, learn what triggers them and learn how to process the emotion that emanates from them. There is no wrong way to do it. And learning it now is always the perfect time.

Remember that you are using the only tool that was ever given to you—your map—to dictate the today version of your life. Creating awareness around what drives you, what engages your map and what challenges you are all possible. Learn what external triggers engage your internal responses. Stop in those moments and ask yourself the question: What am I making this mean? The answers may astound you. Understand the patterns you've collected from childhood. Create enough awareness to change them. Learning to navigate those spaces takes time and is often pretty scary if it's not something you've done before; yet, just like the bike, the more you do it, the more confident you'll become.

We Learn About Ourselves by Experiencing Others

Like a piece of embroidery, everyone has a messy interior. Like learning to ride that bike, remember that today is your first day riding. And if you were trying to create a masterpiece with a broken pencil, how effective and accurate do you believe you would be?

Questions for Insight

➢ Time to flip your pencil over and start editing. If you could use the eraser to remove the biggest challenge on your map, what would you erase? Before you erase all of it, jot down a few things. What's the biggest lesson you learned from that challenge?

_____

_____

_____

➢ What did that lesson allow you to do that would have otherwise been impossible?

_____

_____

_____

➢ When was the first time you remember running that pattern?

_____

_____

_____

➢ Whose voice do you hear when you reflect back on that learned space?

➢ As the today version of you, what do you know now about the energy behind that person's map?

➢ What did your (*insert then aged self*) need to know at that moment?

➢ How can you share that with him/her now?

➤ If you flipped the newly sharpened pencil right
  side up, how could you reframe that story to
  serve you now?

_____

_____

_____

Pause with me. I've been where you are, staring down these
same questions. I didn't wake up this way. I've walked through
hell to get here. I don't share that to get your pity. I share
that to show you that if I can do it, you sure the hell can too!
I promise you without a doubt that my seventeen-year-old
self could never have imagined or dreamt up the version
of Jodee that I am today. It was a step-by-step, next-deci-
sion-by-next-decision process of allowing myself to evolve
over time.

➤ Knowing that, what will be possible for you one year
  from today with a newly edited story?

_____

_____

_____

_____

➢ How about five years from now?

➢ Get crazy and dream ten years out! Who will you be then? What kind of an impact will you make on this world?

➢ What can you start doing right now that makes that journey just a bit sweeter?

➢ What's on your map that might prevent this all from happening?

PART II

The Key to Your Map

Chapter 5

Six Layers of Human Behavior

My guess is that by this point you are starting to uncover a great deal of content on your map that you previously had zero awareness of. As we move into Part II of this book, allow me to create some awareness for you around human behavior and the creation of your map. After spending nearly three decades studying it, one thing I know for sure is that in order to understand human behavior, you must first identify its layers of construct. In these next pages, I will share with you the Six Layers of Human Behavior™ that live on your map, what they are, how they work and which of the key areas will be most helpful in unpacking each layer. The six layers, in an intentional and proper order, are values, beliefs, stories, thoughts, emotions, and actions, outcomes, and behaviors. Each one of these layers play an integral role on your map.

Much like your map, each one of the Six Layers of Human Behavior differs from person to person. Meaning each person has the same structured six layers (values, beliefs, stories, etc.); however, what they value, what they believe and the stories, thoughts, emotions and behaviors they individually create differ from person to person. Keep these six layers in mind as you learn the different modalities throughout this book. Having this frame of reference and comprehending these six layers plays a key role in grasping the next several chapters and the book as a whole. These six layers are also the foundation to the NeuroEnlighten™ method. *The NeuroEnlighten was created by myself as a healing method used to create awareness and to acknowledge and release rooted, and often unconscious, memories from the nervous system.*

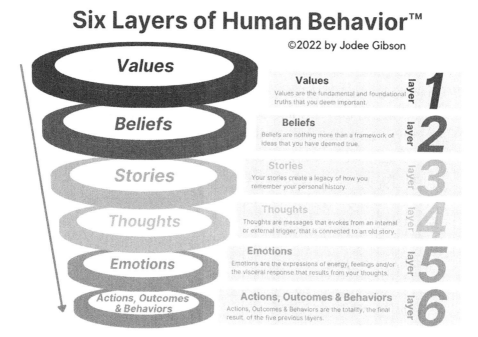

Six Layers of Human Behavior™

©2022 by Jodee Gibson

Values

Beliefs

Stories

Thoughts

Emotions

Actions, Outcomes & Behaviors

Values layer 1
Values are the fundamental and foundational truths that you deem important.

Beliefs layer 2
Beliefs are nothing more than a framework of ideas that you have deemed true.

Stories layer 3
Your stories create a legacy of how you remember your personal history.

Thoughts layer 4
Thoughts are messages that evokes from an internal or external trigger, that is connected to an old story.

Emotions layer 5
Emotions are the expressions of energy, feelings and/or the visceral response that results from your thoughts.

Actions, Outcomes & Behaviors layer 6
Actions, Outcomes & Behaviors are the totality, the final result, of the five previous layers.

The awareness you will gain from understanding these layers opens more access to places that were previously either functioning at an unconscious level or taken as truth. Identifying and isolating these six layers helps you create awareness around where the challenge lies—is it a value that's being challenged, is it a belief that is limited, etc. The more you understand about each layer, the more access you will have to yourself, your map and your future. Each one of these layers is described briefly below and then more in-depth in future chapters. Coincidentally, there are Six Layers of Human Behavior, and there are also six key areas or modalities that can be used to edit these layers, as well as your map. Stay focused and understand the difference.

Values

Think of your values as your internalized compass. Values are the fundamental and foundational truths that you deem important. They are what draw you toward or away from things. Values emanate from your childhood experiences and are directly connected to the things you experience in your environment—your family norms, your social circles, your religious beliefs, your educational exposure, your cultural norms—as well as all the things that you have deemed as normal.

Values impact the way you communicate and the way you make decisions. They create discernment and establish your boundaries around *that's wrong* or *this is right*. Your values grow from being repeatedly exposed to people, places and things. They are the spaces that bring about frustration for you when they are out of alignment and are also responsible for producing certainty for you when they are in alignment. The alignment of your values is what your passion thrives on. Your values alone are the biggest guiding principles of your life and build the foundation of your map.

Beliefs

Although values and beliefs can feel like they are looped into each other, they are two completely different things. Beliefs are founded in values. Beliefs are built over time from repetitive attempts, exposures or impactful imprints and are nothing more than a framework of ideas that you have deemed true. Beliefs consistently seek out agreements for validation. You do this as a soothing mechanism, at a highly unconscious level, in order to validate your (emotional, physical or mental) safety. While beliefs may take time to build, they can be changed in an instant. Your beliefs establish your perspective (it's too loud in here, that's too far away, I'm a great artist). Beliefs are the map, and reality is the territory. The more you experience both your values and your beliefs, the more you normalize the patterns and the outcomes they create.

Stories

Stories are the containers that house your memories. They are filtered through and founded in your values and your beliefs, and they become the storyline of your map. Your stories build a legacy of how you remember your personal history. The more heightened an emotion was at the time, the more impactful the stories are remembered. Your map houses your stories. Your stories are the exact space that your thoughts emanate from, and all too often, your stories limit. Although you have one main life story that is individually yours, there are a myriad of stories inside that main story. Much like your beliefs, the powerful stories you tell yourself become normalized over time and run on default.

The more you repeat your old stories and recycle your old emotions, the more you loop things together that truly may have never been connected. The constant retelling and over-lapping details simply start to run together. The challenge with stories is that oftentimes you feel stuck in a story, con-tained without options. Know that that stuck energy is not as a result of the first time you experienced the story, rather it is a result of the compound effects or symptoms you continue to experience from the rooted, unprocessed trauma and the beliefs you have produced by retelling and reliving the story again and again and again.

Thoughts

Thoughts are the message that evokes from an internal or ex-ternal trigger— you feel something, you hear something, you see something, you smell something, you taste something— that is connected to an old story. That trigger awakens your map and engages an old story. Because you spend so much time retelling your stories, thoughts are most often an old memory versus a newly formed idea. Thoughts are the culmi-nation of your values, your beliefs and your story. Each one of your thoughts invites and evokes an emotional response.

To stop the thoughts, you must first identify the origin of the story. Once you have awareness of where your thoughts emanate from, only then can you choose them freely. Until that occurs, you are simply living in a default state, trying to see new parts of the territory while navigating around with an old, outdated map. Because you have normalized your map, your values, your beliefs and your stories, they will not feel out of place or even responsible for your behavior once it occurs. Quite the opposite is true; once the previous four layers are healed, what grows from that space are healthy, productive intentional thoughts.

Emotions

Emotions are the expressions of energy and feelings and the visceral response that results from your thoughts. The level of intensity of an emotion that is felt is completely dependent upon the initial experience you had with that exact emotion. The way in which an emotion enters your body is the way in which you will forever recall it, if and until you intentionally change it. This means you will forever store and recall emotions in the way in which you learned them until you purposely learn them differently. Your emotions are tied directly to your boundaries, your expectations, and your awareness. As you begin to master this space, you will uncover the notion that your emotions are 100 percent a decision (consciously or unconsciously). Uncontrollable emotions often come as a result of unprocessed trauma.

The reason some emotions feel so heavy while others feel so light is all dependent upon the thoughts and stories they emanate from. When your map has deep emotions (energy) anchored in different stories, it often feels impossible to change, shift or experience anything other than where you are stuck. The story you are continually and unconsciously retelling simply validates or confirms the thought, and the cycle repeats, intensifying the emotion. Depending upon how deeply looped your responses are, your awareness around your decisions was probably not even evident until now. Your thoughts invite and evoke emotional responses. The tools provided herein teach you how to master your emotions.

Actions, Outcomes & Behaviors

Actions, outcomes and behaviors are the totality of the five previous layers. Behavior comes as a direct result of the values, beliefs, stories, thoughts and emotions that you are processing and as the end result of that chain reaction. Unbeknownst to you, your actions, outcomes and behaviors are very telling of what your previous five layers are housing. Your behaviors come as a result of the roots and the story they're founded in. They are the final product and not really editable from that last layer. As you will learn in future chapters, attempting to change, medicate, alter or stop a behavior is often incredibly ineffective. Change starts from the top. Actions, outcomes and behaviors are the external action or reaction to your internal processing. The majority of these behaviors are simply learned, patterned, neurological responses. To edit this final layer, you have to start with the layer above it and work backwards until you identify where the thread line started.

Using the Six Layers for Guidance

One thing I know for sure is the more fluent and conscious you become of your six layers, the more you can purposely and consciously impact not only yourself but also the world. These anchored values, beliefs and stories on your map are the exact things that stay in the way of your success because this is the map that you are unknowingly using to navigate the territory. Most of the content collected on your map lies dormant until it's triggered (internally or externally). Because your brain seeks efficiency, it builds an unconscious response pattern, and you normalize your actions, outcomes and behaviors. You repeat behaviors to satisfy your beliefs, similar to confirmation bias. Behaviors reinforce beliefs and the loop cycles again. Reliving what happened yesterday becomes an unconscious cycle and is completely unnecessary. Your future is ahead of you. Focus that way.

As you dive into the next chapters, use the knowledge and placement of these six layers as guidance. The more fluent you become in each of these areas, the more access you have to mastering your thoughts, your emotions and the outcomes they create. The hierarchy of the Six Layers of Human Behavior are consistent and will not change. The only additional thing that may create space between each layer is the presence of confirmation bias. Confirmation bias is when you seek out and find things in the world that support your map, your values and your beliefs, further validating that you are correct. This allows you to believe you made the right choice and there is evidence of that all around you. Confirming your thoughts, acknowledging your actions and feeling validated about them is how loops are created.

Take note that confirmation bias is a two-way street. It will validate and confirm things for you even when those things are not healthy or in alignment with where you are headed.

What keeps people outside of their goals or their ideal performance is rarely skill level, yet almost always the thoughts and the level of energy (LOE) with which they approach them. The things you value, the beliefs you hold and the stories they tell create a trickle-down effect for your thoughts, your emotions, and your actions, outcomes and behaviors. It's simply an equation. Your map becomes the sum total. You are not a victim of your map. It's simply a recorded moment in time, and it's absolutely editable.

Using the Six Layers of Human Behavior as a guide, these next seven chapters will introduce six key areas and modalities that can be used to edit your layered map. As you read through the balance of Part II, things may sound redundant. Things may repeat. Things may not apply. Things may get uncomfortable. Things may feel flippant, confusing or out of order. Things may provoke you. And there may be times when things may not make sense. All of this is normal. Each one of our maps was created in a different time, with different trusted voices, and with a plethora of different things to value and believe. Each map is completely different. Honor how each piece of this book speaks to those differences.

Each one of the modalities listed below are presented in future chapters. They are presented in as much detail as necessary to edit the respective layer of your map. Use the chart below to identify which modality can be used to edit each layer.

And lastly, indulge yourself. Play full out. Identify your values. Challenge your beliefs. Embrace what makes sense. Release what does not serve you and trust the process. You are a beautiful human, and you are quite possibly the only thing standing in your way.

Tools Used to Infiltrate the Six Layers of Human Behavior™

VALUES

— Neuro Linguistic Programming (NLP)

— Levels of Energy (LOE)

— Trauma & Emotional Development

— Anchors & Triggers

BELIEFS

— Neuro Linguistic Programming (NLP)

— Levels of Energy (LOE)

— Trauma & Emotional Development

— Anchors & Triggers

STORY

— Neuro Linguistic Programming (NLP)

— Levels of Energy (LOE)

— Trauma & Emotional Development

— Interrupt the Story™

— Anchors & Triggers

THOUGHTS

— Neuro Linguistic Programming (NLP)

— Levels of Energy (LOE)

— Trauma & Emotional Development

— Interrupt the Story™

— Anchors & Triggers

EMOTIONS

— Neuro Linguistic Programming (NLP)

— Levels of Energy (LOE)

— Trauma & Emotional Development

— Anchors & Triggers

ACTIONS, OUTCOMES & BEHAVIORS

— Neuro Linguistic Programming (NLP)

— Unpacking the five previous layers

Chapter 6

The Key to Your Map

Anything outside of your awareness is outside of your control.

Your Awareness

Your map represents your model of the world. It represents the collection of experiences you've had previous to today. It includes your values, your beliefs, your stories, your thoughts, your emotions, and all the actions, outcomes and behaviors that come from those spaces. This includes the level of consciousness, the anchors, the triggers, the buttons and what keeps those things attached to you. It reveals your past traumas, your ability to self-regulate and how you've become this version of yourself.

Think about your map as a kaleidoscope, it's like looking at every piece of your life all pulled together and viewed through one lens. That lens—your map—skews the territory by pulling it in through your personalized kaleidoscope, creating your individual perspective. Each of those layers was personally created by you. From that subjective space, your map reveals how you feel about yourself, how you feel about others, how you feel about relationships, money, education, family, time, etc. It reveals what you value, what you view as important, your level of humility and your ability to be vulnerable—or not to be. It literally houses every single piece of you. The more committed you become to your map, the less of the territory you will actually experience.

This book is designed to create a fundamental understanding of the Six Layers of Human Behavior and the six key areas that create sustainable holistic healing. In the next six chapters, you will learn all the modalities necessary to begin understanding and editing your map, including

➢ Neuro Linguistic Programming (NLP): Chapter 7

➢ the TEA Coaching Model: Chapter 8

➢ Consciousness and the Levels of Energy (LOE): Chapter 9

➢ the Presence of Anchors and Triggers: Chapter 10

➢ the Powerful Stories We Tell Ourselves: Chapter 11

➢ Interrupt the Story™: Chapter 12

➢ Trauma, Emotional Development and Arrested Emotional Development: Chapter 13.

You will learn about the world of NLP, values and map building. You will learn about how behaviors are created through thoughts, emotions and actions (TEA), how TEA creates loops, where emotions are born and how behaviors are built. You will learn about thoughts and stories that keep our addictive loop responses cycling. You will learn about levels of consciousness, the structure of expansion and contraction, and the law of vibration (deeper than the laws of attraction). You will learn about anchors and triggers and what attracts us to all those spaces. You will learn about the powerful stories we tell ourselves and learn how to Interrupt the Story. And finally, you will learn about emotional development, emotional regulation, and how the presence of trauma can create emotional dysregulation and arrested emotional development.

With the information in this book, you will learn the skills necessary to heal your map. Although each one of these is a discipline inside itself, the compound effect they create when layered together establishes a force to be reckoned with. With your healed map, your success becomes inevitable. Before you dive all the way in, a brief synopsis of each is available below.

Understanding NLP

Your map is deeply layered in emotion. Your emotional responses have been layered in and were acquired over time and have now become normalized and just run on default. You never assume any of these responses are in your control. Learning your map allows you to establish some awareness of the values, beliefs, stories and thoughts that create the emotions you often feel contained by. The foundation of NLP is a great tool to use to build this awareness. Working with a Licensed NLP Practitioner or Licensed NLP Trainer to build the awareness and access necessary for change is how you gain control of your responses.

I used the word licensed intentionally as NLP is not a regulated or protected space. There are a myriad of people and organizations teaching it incorrectly. Know who you are learn-ing it from.

Remember that anything outside of your awareness is out-side of your control. Awareness creates access. The more you understand, the more access you gain over your layers and your map. Over time, instead of succumbing to the things that used to run unconsciously, you will start using your map con-sciously and with great intention, embracing your responses and gaining access to all the things you need.

Your map reveals what makes you tick, what makes you grin and what engages your passion. It also reveals where the old wounds are, how they still affect you and what you use to mask them. You project into the world what you see on your map. If there's shame on your map, you will shame others. If there's blame, you will look for people or things to point to externally. If there's justification and rationalization, you will look for ways to manipulate and justify the facts. If there's compassion, you will spend your time trying to fix things and others. If there's acceptance, you will find peace with what is. If you can access your intuition, you will look for ways to connect with others, creating synergy. If you are enlightened, you will look to enlighten others.

The key is to understand how these patterns show up on your map. First, identify how these default perspectives and organic responses are attached to each layer of your map. Second, recognize that your perspective and your layers are where your power lies on your map currently. Third, when you can gain awareness of the different layers, you can begin to recognize which of these make you contract and which ones make you expand. This awareness of the ability to choose to expand versus to contract forever changes your life, your layers and your map.

Judgment contracts you; curiosity expands you. Shame contracts you; acceptance expands you. Blame contracts you; connection expands you. Guilt, anger, fear, anxiety, frustration and aggression all contract you. Kindness, sensitivity, wisdom, joy, creativity and optimism all expand you.

Understanding Consciousness— Expand & Contract

When your body contracts, it literally stops flowing. Your energy stops flowing. From this contracted space you cannot grow, you cannot absorb and you cannot function as a whole person. Your body has shifted into survival mode and is pumping copious amounts of cortisol and adrenaline into your system. Adrenaline starts flowing and your body is in a state of arrest. You are stuck. Things around you may grow and external things may soothe your pain, yet internally you will remain stuck until you can shift out of this survival mode response. This is the beginning of arrested development. More on this in chapter 9.

The other side of that coin is when your body expands. When your body expands it literally releases, relaxes and allows things to flow. From that space, your energy is fluid. Endorphins saturate your brain, and your body is in coherence. It is from this expanded state that you can mature and evolve. It's from this expanded space that your brain sets off serotonin, dopamine and all the happy chemicals that saturate your brain. From this space, you attract healthy abundance into your life. Because you have released the contracted energy, your level of energy rises and you begin attracting new opportunities, relationships and experiences that are full of this lighter, expanded energy.

Both spaces, expanded and contracted, attract like things to them. Contracted energy attracts contracted heavy energy. Expanded energy attracts expanded enlightened energy. This is the exact space that Napoleon Hill teaches from. Knowing which things on your map pull forward these different responses is where your power lies. The lists for both sides, expanded and contracted, are endless; yet learning how they are all intricately interwoven into our map and how they show up as we move through the territory (world) is key. The more you learn about your map, the more you will understand the story behind those said spaces, become fluent in what's anchored to them and know what engages them.[7]

Your childhood experiences were interpreted, internalized and encoded onto your map by your understanding of the territory at the time. These spaces became intertwined decades ago, deep inside your childhood, and over time you have simply created patterned loops and normalized them. Today they still reside in their expanded or contracted states and have taken up permanent residence on your map.

Understanding & Spilling TEA

Your experiences then create the awareness around your **T**houghts, **E**motions and **A**ctions (TEA) that house your belief system. These are the beliefs that you establish as factual versus experiential. You may have had one bad experience in a certain area and have now sworn off that whole area, embracing the idea that *X* is bad. Having an experiential view would mean understanding that you did in fact have a bad experience, yet it was an isolated event where you had limited access to fundamental resources. If you stay committed to the first "factual" event, you will seek out things on your path that create alignment with your juxtaposed layer—*see, I told you*, or *this always happens* and other common phrases—that validate your map. This is called confirmation bias. You spend your days trying to prove your map, to be seen, to be validated or to be defined.

The other side of this example leans into the experiential side. You stay curious in the spaces that previously felt *bad*, knowing that if you revisit them again from an expansive view, maybe something different will happen and a new TEA will emerge. Know that the language you create around these spaces draws in the people you connect with. Your language builds your map. Your thoughts build your map. Your energy builds your map.

Understanding Anchors & Triggers

Over the course of your life, you have unknowingly installed multiple anchors onto your map that are often unconsciously triggered in your daily life. An anchor is essentially the foundational root cause or experience that becomes a permanent fixture on your map and is awakened by an unintentional trigger (internal or external), engaging a patterned, familiar response. You continually build your map daily and reinforce the layers that reside on it, both consciously and unconsciously. You knowingly and unknowingly align yourself with people who have similar maps, similar beliefs and similar energy. Know that redesigning and editing your map is just as easy as reinforcing it. It just takes intentional effort.

Your map reveals the emotions that you keep anchored down deep inside your story. The lessons you learn and the things that are added to your map are not who you are, they're simply where you've been. If you survived child neglect or spousal abuse or fleeing from your native country or even war, you are not those things. They simply hold a place on your map and as soon as you decide to release the energy around them, they no longer define who you are.

The lessons you learn and the things that are added to your map are not who you are, they're simply where you've been.

Take a moment and create some conscious awareness around a few of your most emotionally engaging anchors—the ones that immediately hijack your emotions as soon as they are mentioned.

Stay consciously aware of how this word, memory or sight engages your neurology and your physiology. As you move through this book, use the tools found within and start unpacking the energy around this memory.

Powerful Stories We Tell Ourselves

Knowing that each thought you think emanates from a story, most often a powerful story. The culmination of your life, your history and all the layers of your map have left a legacy in its wake. That legacy, over time, becomes a story. The more heightened the emotion, the more powerful the story. These are the exact spaces that your thoughts emanate from. Understanding the powerful stories you live inside and creating conscious awareness around what happens in your body when you recall that moment is how change happens. Recalling that memory (like the one you jotted down above), that sound, that taste, that picture, that emotion or that day, and then taking a moment and consciously asking yourself the question: "what am I making this mean?" leads you direct-ly to the places that continually keep you feeling *stuck*.

Deep down inside, you have internalized a meaning, a storyline, or an emotion from your first experience with that memory, not from today. Your reaction or your response to today's event simply triggers that old emotional, unprocessed wound. Be still and create conscious awareness of what's coming up. Slow down and engage with your neurology. Resilience is the ability to tell your story without being inside your story. It's about allowing your body and your mind to be disconnected from the story because you've processed it and allowed yourself to move through it, releasing the destructive energy it held on your map and inside you. This is the begin-ning of emotional regulation.

The map creates awareness for us that all the behaviors we are trying to interrupt started with a pattern. If your neurology is still responding, the patterns still exist. In this book, I will teach you several modalities that allow you access to edit the patterns and layers that create them, essentially healing your map. Embrace the idea that your map is the tool you get to learn from. It's not about the character flaw we observe in ourselves or in others. It's about the idea that part of our map was created with a broken pencil. You may be holding judgment around who you needed that person to be or how you needed them to respond rather than allowing them to be who they were in that moment. Allow yourself to view it with pure and utter curiosity. Ask yourself: What is happening on their map that would cause this action to make sense to them? Or ask: What did my then-year-old self need to know at that moment? Then take a moment to speak to that version of you.

Remember back to how old you were for the memory that's coming forward. Where did that child feel safe? Offer to meet them in that safe space and share what you know now. Offer support and guidance, letting them know that their voice and their presence matters and that you can take it from here. Allow that younger version of you to heal and know that they are now protected by an adult (you). Over time the energy from that space will begin to dissipate. That old energy may pop up at a later age and the same exercise can be used to clear that old energy. This opens a whole new world of constructive, forward-moving energy.

Your map reveals the history of the layers from which you were built and from which you operate. Know that you are simply using the only tool that was ever given to you—your map. Your map reveals what that toolbox looks like in the present day. The map is not the territory means that the way you remember things isn't always the way they were. It's simply the way you interpret them through your map and your layers. If you remember a time as an eight-year-old child when you were being disciplined by your parents, you may recall feelings of hurt, sadness, embarrassment, shame and abandonment. Backing up and taking a 30,000-foot view today allows you to absorb the idea that although your parents may or may not have had the best disciplining techniques, the motivation behind their actions was in some capacity to keep you safe. In that moment in time, you pulled forward an eight-year-old's emotion, which is all you had access to. If that disciplining moment was traumatic for you, it established the foundation of your layers and was deeply encoded onto your map. Today, when those feelings are provoked, they're still eight years old. The button was encoded and anchored in the emotion of an eight-year-old.

It's possible you may already be a parent yourself at this point. Knowing what you know now, what other things could you allow yourself to believe around that old, anchored memory? As a parent, is it ever your intention to make your child feel hurt, sad, embarrassed, ashamed or abandoned? Probably not. Yet in these present-day moments, you can only use what's available to you. Odds are high that you may pull forward your eight-year-old emotions as you try to discipline your own children. That is because you are using the only thing you have access to—the layers of your map. Without conscious awareness of the ineffective layers, this will forever live on your map and the maps of your children and their children until someone interrupts the pattern. This is how generational trauma pervades.

Know that there is zero judgment here, just clear, utter awareness of all the things that your map reveals. You may not be aligned with your best self in every given moment, yet your intentions are always pure. In the moments when you feel out of alignment or out of control, that's when you start drawing with a broken pencil, leaving remnants of your misaligned self. Remember that your map is editable.

These are prime examples of what your map reveals. You cannot fix what's outside of you. You can only shift the way in which you interpret what you observe, which is why learning about all the things that are encoded into the layers of your map is vital. Healing your map is a mind-body connection. Understanding how and why your body responds to the world around you is how you get closer to the best version of yourself.

Also, it's quite possible that you get so committed to your map that you miss the territory altogether. You walk around with your map literally covering your eyes, blinded by all your previous experiences, unable to take in new information instead of setting the map down and getting super curious about what's possible now. What would be possible if you were free from your previous memories? Think about how many layers deep the memories are that pull forward so much pain. How would you take the territory in with a clean map and stash of fresh pencils? Think about a lotus flower—you can grow from anywhere once you decide you're ready.

Understanding Trauma & Emotional Regulation

Your map reveals your childhood. Like many of us, your map may have been built inside childhood trauma. Whether it was one huge trauma or a million microtraumas, these past experiences shape the way we show up in the world (territory). Each and every experience you've had has become encoded on your map. The traumatic ones left a deeper groove. Know that the more heightened an experience, the deeper the anchor it leaves. Someone in your past created an anchor, or you interpreted a space, that left you helpless, unattached and unable to access emotional stability or express your authenticity. This created deep deficits and major contracted energy on your map. It created powerful anchors that are now set off by the slightest triggers. It created layers that are rooted in shame, rooted in anger or rooted in sadness. Know that this is not always about healing every single piece of the trauma; it may be about simply allowing the recognition of it and knowing it doesn't have to be in charge anymore.

Your map reveals your default level of consciousness. Again, like water, energy self-levels. You seek out the same energy and the same consciousness that you were built with. You unintentionally seek out the same level of consciousness of the environment that built you. You may seek out drama because that's the only language your nervous system speaks. You may seek out people who allow you to retreat and hide because that's the norm for you. You may seek out angry, rowdy, disconnected or emotionally unavailable people because that's the fluent language your map has been encoded with, and you feel right at home in those spaces. There are a multitude of other examples that can have a normalized presence on your map without your knowledge. If you are curious about what your default level is, look at your phone, your friends, the music you listen to and the clothes you wear; examine the things you eat, the books you read and the things you watch on television. Those are all indicators of where your energy is. These are the things that lead directly to the culture of you.

When all those things are present and you have normalized the world they create around you, it can be challenging to imagine a life without them; yet rarely do you realize that these are the exact things keeping you outside of your ideal outcome. I know that was a loaded statement. Reread it if necessary. Is your *culture of you* really in alignment with who you are trying to be? Does it help you be the best version of yourself, or is it masking who you are, allowing you to hide or minimize your presence? These are the things that you will find on your map. If this is not in alignment with your desired outcome, it's a great place to start creating some change, shifting some energy and establishing new intentional layers.

Awareness Equals Access

Another interesting thing you will find on your map is your vices. Everyone has a vice, maybe two or three. Examining your vices and understanding what role they play, what they are attached to and what they soothe provides incredible insight. Coming from a person who was consistently traumatized as a child, one of my greatest vices was humor. Humor was the largest shield I could find that was always accessible. We use shields to protect us from feeling emotions we cannot process; however, it's these same shields that keep us outside of healthy relationships. Present day, I leverage humor for the same reason. It is the best icebreaker available, and it makes the most challenging conversations so much easier. It cuts through pain and allows people to find lightness in themselves and in the people around them.

Odds are high you may not be able to put your finger on a vice right this moment but give it some time. The more awareness you have the easier they are to find. Most people have no awareness of the things they use to soothe their nervous system. As one of my favorite humans, Dr. Rao Kolusu often shares, you are aware of everything else around you except for yourself. Understanding the vices you use to soothe yourself leads you directly to the things you want to change. Do you run off and go smoke? Do you reach for a drink? Do you head to the store, take a nap, retreat and find solace, ring a friend and vent? There is a myriad of things you might do in order to soothe that energy. Take a moment and jot down where your energy goes when your feelings start intensifying. The more you write, the more awareness you build.[8]

_____

_____

_____

_____

_____

_____

_____

Understanding your map with all its vices, layers, TEA and experiences as well as understanding the maps of others allows you to create a space of curiosity around the differences in our maps versus jumping to judgment. Remember that curiosity expands you and judgment contracts you. If you are afraid to tell someone something because you fear their judgment, you are basing that opinion on your current map and any prior experience you've had with this person. Know that when you share something with someone, they filter that information through their map. If they choose to judge you, to disagree or to be upset, it's about their map, not yours. It's simply about the idea that the information you are supplying does not align with their map. It has nothing to do with you. HARD STOP.

Remember that it's not right or wrong, it's just different. Neither of you are right at that moment, nor are you wrong. You simply have two different maps from which you are building your perspectives. Two different sets of layers. Two wildly different kaleidoscopes trying to describe the same territory. It may also spark the question: Why are you trying to navigate my world with your map? Your meaning is your meaning, and your story is your story. When you take your meaning and your story and you try to figure out what someone else is saying from your map, it makes complete sense that things get lost in translation.

The powerful awareness you gain from stepping back and creating awareness around different maps allows you to create a fundamental understanding. It brings you back to the fact that you simply don't know what you don't know. Learning to navigate through this world (the territory) personally, with a new, updated map, and socially, by staying curious about other people's maps, just makes life easier.

It's like the nonparents who walk around making judgments on parents and saying things like *well when I'm a parent, my kids are going to X.* Then they become a parent and their maps immediately change. They adjust, they actualize, and then they realize their previous map was incomplete. It was missing the integral information needed to make an accurate decision. Now that they have that information, they know what they know, and their perspective changes. They clearly didn't know then what they do know now.

Your map reveals what you value. If you believe someone likes you or doesn't like you for a specific reason, that's about your map and about what you value. Remember value is the first and most impactful layer of your map. If you think someone loves you because of how wealthy you are, that's because you value wealth, or the lack thereof. If you look down on others because of their lack of financial resources, that's about you and your values, not the person you are judging. If you believe someone likes you because you are physically attractive or very fit, odds are high that you value the exterior qualities that make someone physically attractive and fit. If you believe someone likes you because you are smart, it's because you value your education. You get the idea. All these examples and so many more all come directly from the layers of your map, your personalized kaleidoscope. One of my favorite quotes is from an African proverb: "Your perception of me is a reflection of you, my response to you is a reflection of me." So powerful and so true. Your response to someone's opinion of you is more important than their opinion.

Your response to someone's opinion of you is more important than their opinion.

What your map reveals are your foundational layers—the multiple, in-depth, very personalized layers that construct the today version of you. In order to show up as your best self, you first have to understand and have access to what makes you your best self. If something is hindering that access, responding as your best self may not be possible. As you start to uncover these spaces, questions like did I choose this or did someone else put this on my map will surface.

Questions for Insight

➢ What things have you identified on your map that you were not previously aware of?

➢ Did you choose that response or did someone else put it on your map?

➢ What belief does this old response serve?

➤ What else could you allow yourself to believe that is
more effective?

_____

_____

_____

_____

➤ What are some of your vices? Are they healthy or
unhealthy? What's the secondary gain you get from
having that vice? (Mine was emotional protection.
I used humor to protect myself because I was
emotionally dysregulated and did not know how to
use my voice appropriately.)

_____

_____

_____

➤ What's the most important layer that is juxtaposed
from your map or the most glaring thing you'd like
to remove, add or edit?

_____

_____

_____

_____

Chapter 7

Understanding NLP

Everything is first a neurological
response . . . and then a decision.
—DR RICHARD BANDLER

The art of NLP began in the late 1970s with the duo Bandler
and Grinder studying language and human behavior at
the deepest levels. Dr. Bandler was a graduate student who
approached Dr. Grinder, a professor of linguistics, in hopes
of validating his intuition. For years, the pair had the luxury
of witnessing, observing and shadowing the then masters of
psychology Virginia Satire, Fritz Perls, and Milton Erickson.
As the co-creators of NLP, Dr. Richard Bandler and Dr. John
Grinder began studying the language and pattern structure of
the clients they were observing. They uncovered something
no one had yet to pick up on: most psychologists and psy-
chotherapists' focus was on the actual challenge the client
was experiencing versus the structure of how it was consistently created. Both Bandler and Grinder were hyper-focused

on what people were doing versus attempting to *fix* the end result.[9]

Up and until that point, no one was taking the time to understand and disassemble how these challenges were consistently being constructed and how they now play a role in your deeply layered map. Bandler and Grinder both began to focus on exactly that, the pattern—the series of decisions that created the consistent behavior versus the actual behavior. From that space, neuro linguistic programming was born.[10]

Before you dive all the way in, allow me to take a moment and break down each word, providing incredible insight.

N Is for Neuro

When you hear the word neuro you may think of the brain, yet neuro actually refers to your entire neurology. You have billions of neurons throughout your entire body. These neurons have been and will continue to be programmed for decades. Your neurology is responsible for how you respond to the world around you, using your five senses. You feel things. You hear things. You see things. You smell things. And you taste things. Those five senses are often referred to as **KAVOG**.

> **K** is kinesthetic—to feel.
>
> **A** is auditory—to hear.
>
> **V** is visual—to see.
>
> **O** is olfactory—to smell.
>
> **G** is gustatory—to taste.

In the world of NLP, these five senses are referred to as your representational systems. Because your neurology has taken the world in through these five systems, you have built your layered map accordingly, encoding each and every memory in one of these five representational systems (senses). In the present day, when you recall a memory, it is encoded in the representational system that it was originally recorded in—the smell of crayons takes you back to elementary school; the sound of the bell ringing means it's time to go home; the thought of homework makes you cringe; and the last day of school represents freedom. The reason this happens is because you had access to these five senses well before you had access to words. The way you learned to process information, previous to having access to language, was through your five representational systems.

Even once you acquired language, you still encoded your experiences and used the original neural pathways to process information. This occurred because there were experiences that, although you had access to language, you simply could not contextualize. Due to this, your neurology leaned into the system it was most fluent in, your five representational systems, and encoded it accordingly. All the information you took in and continue to take in is encoded in a representational system.

This is why you can walk through your local convenience store and all of a sudden smell fifth grade. It's why a song can come on the radio and immediately provoke a strong emotion. And it's precisely why the smell from that ER will forever live in my neurology. The reintroduction of the same KAVOG that a memory was originally encoded in immediately takes you back to the exact moment it was encoded on your map, and you reexperience the same visceral memory all over again. Rarely is there a warning alerting you to what lies ahead. There is also no awareness when a KAVOG-encoded memory implants into your neurology. That sound, that smell, that feeling, that taste or that visual glimpse immediately cues your neurology up for a reenactment, emotions and all. That KAVOG response is deeply anchored to your layered map.

Words also provoke our neurology. Words, smells, tastes, sounds and visual cues all evoke awareness. Over time and at a highly unconscious level, you create patterns that align with these responses. Think of what happens in your dog's neurology when you mention the word *walk*. Even if you're sharing with him that you cannot go for a walk right now because you're busy working or you will take him for a walk later, it does not matter what words come before or after *walk*. Once the word is spoken, his neurology is ready to go! The same goes for a child (or maybe even for you) once the ringing bells of the ice cream truck roll past. It's kind of like trying to put out a five-alarm fire with a bottle of water. Your neurology works the same. The more you run a pattern, the more fluent the neural pathway becomes. The more fluent the pathway, the more it runs on default. Eventually, the response becomes who you are. This is neuroplasticity simplified.

L Is for Linguistics

Linguistics are the awareness and interpretation you have around language, the way you communicate and the meaning you give to that communication. Linguistics are also the language you give to the audible experiences that you have internalized. Linguistics are verbal and nonverbal sounds. They are nonword noises, including pace, tempo, flow, cadence, volume, etc. Linguistics is the meaning you create around the things you experience. It is what happens when you observe that someone's audio does not match their video. It's what you observe when someone verbally says yes and their physiology clearly says no. Linguistics are about what you experience when people speak and how you respond to it.

Linguistics are largely interpretational and vary widely. Although we all would universally agree that this book is written in English, we do not have a universal agreement about what each word inside the English language means. Due to that, your definition of the words you experience is left to your interpretation. Only 9 percent of communication is spoken word, much of it gets lost in interpretation and translation. Could it be that we are all communicating with the same words yet trying to convey something completely different? Or quite the opposite, could it also be that we are communicating with different words while trying to convey the same idea? Knowing that, how much of your linguistic content could be misconstrued on an ongoing basis? The clarity created here is that if only 9 percent of communication is spoken word, much of it gets lost in interpretation and translation.

P Is for Programming

Programming refers to your ability to organize your communication and neurology to achieve a specific outcome. It's the way you have programmed your brain and also the way you have allowed it to be programmed over the years. Knowing that people now shy away from the word programming, remember that NLP was created in the late 1970s and early 1980s, back when computers were being built. According to Dr. Bandler, programming was a very cool word back then. My guess is that if NLP was created today, P would stand for patterning. For all intents and purposes, allow your brain to replace the word programming with patterning.[11]

Because your brain is wired for efficiency, it operates inside of millions of patterns. Remember, you have thought patterns, emotional patterns, linguistic patterns, behavioral patterns, etc. Although efficiency is what keeps you alive, many of the patterns you are operating with emanate from the layers of your map built from your childhood. You have been building your map from day one. Each and every day you repeat hundreds of patterns, regardless of their efficiency. Your brain is a pattern-making machine. You think in patterns. You respond in patterns. You soothe in patterns. You behave in patterns. You learn in patterns. You have thousands of effective patterns that keep you alive and out of trouble, yet you also have thousands of outdated patterns that keep you outside of your goals. Think neuroplasticity. The more you use a neural pathway, the more embedded and normal it becomes in your neurology and the more you normalize it.

Think of it this way, if you already know how to walk, would it be challenging to walk differently? If you already know how to breathe, would it be challenging to breathe differently? And if you already know how to think and process information, would it be challenging to learn how to think differently? The answer is absolutely! You are operating with the same core foundational, neurological responses and beliefs that were created and encoded onto your map well before you made it to middle school. It's from this exact space that your values are built. Kathleen La Valle expands on the idea that the more you run a pattern, it eventually builds a belief; and the more times you experience that belief, it solidifies a value. These spaces are cyclical. The more you experience both your values and beliefs, the more you undoubtedly normalize the patterns and the outcomes they create regardless of their validity.[12]

Normalizing the Map

Odds are high you have no concept or capacity to think outside of these spaces that you've built and normalized over time. When trying to affect change, you may struggle to find the pattern; nothing stands out because this is the way it's always been. Thinking about this idea like your computer or your smartphone, how often does your device demand that you install the latest update? I'm guessing that if you want your device to run at the highest level of efficiency, the answer is once every few months, and with certainty it's at least annually. Without installing the updates, your device will eventually lose efficiency, may start glitching, or may simply stop working altogether. Some apps may even refuse to open or acclimate without the necessary updates.

Using that same concept, how efficient is your current map? Odds are high that you have unknowingly been using the same patterns from childhood, pulled from your outdated layered map. The question becomes how effective are these patterns today at taking you towards your desired outcome. When was the last time you investigated and or updated the values, beliefs, and patterns that you are building your life with?

Let's recap.

Neuro → The way your body responds

Linguistic → to the observed language around you and

Programming → the patterns of meanings you create around it.

(unconscious competence)

As Bandler and Grinder began to develop their approach, they realized that amplifying attention and energy on the exact thing someone was trying to minimize—a fear, a limiting belief, or a phobia—made zero sense. They instead focused on studying the things that people did that were successful. They studied the patterns those ideal outcomes emanated from. They focused on successful behaviors, subjective experiences and how people created them. They understood that you are always in a state (of mind) and that the quality of your life is always directly related to the state that you are in. The work of NLP was designed to understand exactly how you get into each state. Two of the main focuses of NLP are your values and your beliefs, the two foundational pieces of the Six Layers of Human Behavior. Values and beliefs both play an integral role in the way you have built and continue to build your layered map.[13]

Bandler and Grinder began to disassemble human behavior, isolating each piece, each belief, each thought, each neurological response, each physiological response, and each decision, conscious or unconscious, as they attempted to understand this process. This granular approach allowed them a different view inside human behavior than ever before. Comparing this perspective to the present day Western psychological approach that believes "much of the activity people experience is from forces beyond their control, forces often assumed as originating outside of the human senses."[14] They began to infiltrate spaces and treat patients whose only other previous option was medication and/or suffering. What they learned was the majority of these behaviors were simply learned patterned neurological responses. Although the symptoms are clearly treatable with medication, soothing a symptom does not change the root cause. Bandler and Grinder's solution to those responses is still, to this day, change work using NLP techniques to treat the root cause, eliminating the need for medication.

The goal with NLP is to identify the responses that effectively create the cause and effect you are seeking and then intentionally duplicate them, creating freedom from the patterns that hinder you. The hope is this will begin to form patterns in other areas of your neurology with familiar neuroplasticity, and vice versa. It's about removing the patterns that are no longer effective or are not allowing you to reach your ideal outcome. Dr. Bandler often explains that the study of NLP is about how you build things inside your mind and then communicate them, first to yourself and then to the world.

Knowing that this is all based on an individual's own respective beliefs and values, allow me to pause and share some information outside of NLP. One of the most fascinating things I have stumbled upon since beginning my studies in human behavior is the idea of imprinting. There's not a ton of information available about it; however, Morris Massey does include it in his work. According to Massey, there are three major periods of life—imprinting, modeling and socialization (more on this later). Although each one of them plays a crucial role, your foundational values are built during the imprinting and early modeling period and beliefs follow. This is a fundamental concept to understanding your first two layers.[15]

Understanding Values

Roy Disney once said, "It's not hard to make decisions when you know what your values are."[16] Values are the fundamental and foundational truths that you deem important. Values emanate from your foundational childhood imprinting experiences. They are connected to the things that you experience in your environment, including your families, your social circles, your religious beliefs, your educational exposure and your cultural norms as well as all the things that you have deemed as normal. Values impact the way you communicate. They impact the way you make decisions and the way you sort information. It's in this space that you develop judgment and begin observing, identifying and possibly vocalizing ideas like *that's wrong*, or *this is the right way*.

Your values grow from being repeatedly exposed to things. Values are the gauges that you use to say yes or no. These are the spaces that are challenged and create frustration for you when they are out of alignment. These are the areas that create certainty for you when they are present and uncertainty when they're not. Your values are what drives your passion. It's important to understand that values alone are your biggest guiding principles and are the most impactful layer of your map.

Much like the points on your map, values differ from person to person. Think of your values as your internalized compass. They guide you without your knowledge or input. Values create discernment for you, and much like the map, they are highly subjective. Regardless of how you're feeling or where your level of emotion is, your values are incredibly consistent. People often want to handpick their values and may vocalize this by saying, "I want to be more into X" or "I really value relationships" or something similar. Allow me to enlighten you, values cannot be handpicked. They emanate from early childhood imprinting and are built on and reinforced by your daily life. If I asked you to make a list of your values right now, odds are incredibly high that the things on that list are not what you truly value.

Let's take a moment and identify your core values. Before moving to step one, grab a pen and write down what you believe to be your values. Once you have them on paper, move to step one.

Step 1: Ask yourself: What do I value most? Jot down the things that you believe you value most in the order that they come up. Remember, there is no right or wrong. The more transparent you allow yourself to be, the more successful you will be. Write down all the things you value. Use a new number for each value.

1. I value. . . family

2. I value. . .

3. I value. . .

Step 2: Working with your answer from step 1, what is it about the first thing on your list that you value most? Record your answers in the column underneath. Although it may sound repetitive, keep going with the same concept and question. Ask yourself that same question for each item on your list. What is it about [insert answer to (1)] that I value most?

1. I value. . . family

    a. Trusted bond

    b.

2. I value . . .

    a.

    b.

3. I value . . .

    a.

    b.

Step 3: Although it may sound repetitive, keep going with the same concept. What is it about [insert answer for (a)] that you value?

1. I value. . . family

   a. Trusted bond

      i. Connection

   b.

      i.

2. I value . . .

   a.

      i.

   b.

      i.

3.

   a.

      i.

   b.

      i.

Continue this process, asking yourself the question, **what is it about that that I value most,** until you find the foundational answer. You will intuitively know when you've found it. If answers keep coming, keep digging. Once the answers stop, challenge them to your best ability and then trust the answer. If the answer feels out of alignment, move on to the next question and circle back later.

Repeat this process for each item you listed from step 1. Take your time. There is no rush. Allow the answers to come up and out in their own time. Revisit this list as often as you need. Know that although values are incredibly powerful, they are also flexible and adjustable with time, awareness and intention.

As you move through this process, start looking for similar themes. My guess is you may have some repeating words that come up in step 2 and in step 3. Feel free to build out a step 4, 5 or 6 if needed. The more granular you get, the more foundational information you will find. You will begin to see patterns in words. As the words begin repeating in steps 2–5 (for each concept), highlight them or pull them out and make a new list. These are your *actual values*, and they create the first layer of your map.

These are your actual values. These values provide a foundational and fundamental list for you to begin creating awareness around. Put them in order and identify if those are the values that will get you where you're trying to go.

Initially, you may have believed that your values were the things you listed in step 1. As you dive deeper, you will be able to uncover the foundations of those concepts, which allows you to properly identify what your values actually are. The next true step is to put them in your order of hierarchy. This is much easier to do with a properly trained NLP Master Practitioner or a Licensed NLP Trainer, as it is challenging to do alone, although not impossible.

Even without putting them in order, seeing them on paper and knowing what is truly driving you gives you the power and direction to make better decisions, to understand yourself at a deeper level and to make sustainable adjustments that create more access for you. Looking at this list now, how much sense does it make that these are the core values running your life? This is what creates your ability to discern what's right and wrong when experiencing the territory. Know that this is an incredibly brief overview of values yet enough to help you build a solid foundation.

Reflecting back to Massey's work, although most of his work may feel a bit out there, I do believe that he was onto something when he described the three major periods. Looking at the role that values play, Massey's three described periods—imprinting, modeling and socialization—make so much sense in this context. The imprinting period is first and occurs from birth to age seven. It's in this period that you begin grouping ideas together and building values. The second period is the modeling period, which occurs from age seven through age fourteen. This is the time when you begin modeling behaviors such as dressing, walking, talking, processing information, accessing feelings, etc., further embedding your values and building beliefs. And lastly, the socialization period from age fourteen through age twenty-one is where you begin to learn how to build relationships, solidifying that first layer and then testing your values and beliefs through action and confirmation.

Understanding Massey's work gives insight into the importance of a child's early imprintable years—what they witness and what they experience is the culmination of who they later become. Kids unconditionally absorb the world (territory) around them and build their value system from that exposure. Remember this is not about judgment in the way that you were parented or the environment that built your value system, yet it is about providing clear and utter awareness around the role those things played for you. Identifying your values, understanding their role, and knowing how they form the world you live in is imperative for intentional self-mastery. Know that as your values were being constructed and confirmed, you began building beliefs around those foundational layers.

Understanding Beliefs

Although values and beliefs can feel like they are looped into each other, they are two completely different things. Beliefs are founded in our values and are built from either repetitive attempts or impactful imprints. For example, if you repeatedly attempt to draw a beautiful picture, yet the results are far from what you deem beautiful, you may, over time, build a belief that you are not a great artist. Or, you may believe that you are an amazing artist and pour your heart and soul into a creation, mesmerized by your ability, only to show it to a friend or family member who scoffs at its appearance, immediately imprinting onto your map that your creation was far from fabulous.

The energy that separates these two examples would be your values. Do you value input from others, or not? If you do, my guess is the words they shared imprinted your map and limited your belief around your artistic abilities, contrary to your initial beliefs. However, if you do not value input from others, you may brush off their comments and stand in your mesmerized state, creating or confirming a belief that you are an amazing artist.

The most powerful thing to learn here is how your values played a role in your life. Did you allow others' words to impact you, or did you decide their words held zero weight, ignoring them and omitting them from your map? This is a pivotal space that often gets overlooked. It's in these moments that you may say things like *he makes me feel bad* or *she said I'm not a good X.* The takeaway here is: Who qualified them to judge your performance? Knowing what you know now, how much sense does it make to give someone else that much power over your map?

If you do value their input, step back and question their ability to judge art. Develop wide-open awareness around how your values not only play a role but also on the impact of that role in the way you live your life. That awareness is what gives you further insight into how you create discernment. If you're projecting the result of that conversation onto the other person and giving your power away, that is a zero-sum game. Someone else cannot change the way you feel. That is a job only for you, and it is solely based on what you allow yourself to value and believe.

Beliefs Are Powerful

Beliefs are also formed over time, resulting from repeated behavior and exposure to the same environments. We repeat behaviors to satisfy our beliefs, which is similar to confirmation bias. Beliefs consistently seek out agreements for validation. We do this as an unconscious soothing mechanism to validate our emotional, physical or mental layers of safety. The interesting thing about beliefs is that although they are powerful, they can change in an instant. As a perfect example, I spent my entire life up to the age of twenty-five being told I wasn't smart. Because of that, I created a foundational belief that aligned with everyone else's map, and I never really applied myself in school. My belief was that it didn't matter how hard I worked, because I wasn't smart.

I vividly remember the day the envelope arrived. I tore it open because it was thinner than what I remembered in previous semesters. As I read the letter it stated that I had been recognized on the dean's list and I fell to tears. Tears of disappointment. Tears of frustration. Tears of sadness. Who was I to think I could go to school? I was busting my ass, using my brain to the fullest capacity, yet it clearly didn't matter. I called my parents sobbing, explaining to them that, although I was doing the best I could, somehow I ended up on the dean's list, a list that I knowingly equated to the principal's list. I literally thought I was in trouble. I thought I was on the principal's list, and I was going to get kicked out of school. I stood in that moment thinking *I am giving it everything I have,* yet *it is clearly not enough.*

I was twenty-five years old, had a seven-year-old daughter and was struggling to finish school. My parents were so supportive on that call, yet they did not understand why I was so upset. It was in that very moment I learned the dean's list was an honor, not a punishment. Yes, you read that right. You see, up until that point, I had no idea what the dean's list was. I was so far removed from smart people I had never even heard of the dean's list. My belief around my ability to learn immediately changed. I almost threw up. At that moment my whole life changed. When people say things like *change takes time* or *change is hard*, I say no! No, ma'am. No, sir. Absolutely not. That change was instantaneous. From that moment forward, my belief around my ability to learn forever changed. Not only did I go on to finish my associate degree with honors, I also completed undergraduate and graduate school, both with honors. Me, the wildly uneducated teen mom.

I share this story for so many reasons. First, if you are a parent and you are building an environment around a child, make sure that environment includes access to the things you are expecting from them. Second, if you are an adult or you are currently working on yourself, know that you have these unassuming, unconscious, unknown layers on your map that were placed there by other people, most likely the trusted voices that helped build your map as a child. This is not about judgment or blame; it's simply about creating awareness around what *is* possible for you outside of what others believe. Success is nothing more than learning information that was previously missing. Trust me when I tell you that anything is possible.

Success is nothing more than learning
information that was previously missing.

I often wonder how different my life would have been if I were raised in a family and educational environment that taught me from day one that I was, in fact, smart or even that I housed the capacity to be smart. Yet I immediately back away from that story because I know that if my life were any different, I would not be where I am today. I honor every single step of my journey. Each piece of my journey was necessary to arrive at this outcome. Everyone's story is given to them for a reason. Beliefs are nothing more than a framework of ideas that you have deemed true. Imagine the things I would never know and the life I would have never lived had I stayed inside the belief that someone else had built around me. What beliefs are you still clinging to that have nothing to do with who you are capable of being?

Beliefs are nothing more than a framework of ideas that you have deemed true.

When you start learning more about NLP and understanding and embracing KAVOG, the idea behind the map is not the territory begins to sink in just a bit more. You start to embrace the idea that each and every part of your life experience has been encoded into your very own layered map. There's a huge awareness that awakens when you realize there is a space between you and your responses. The map allows you to separate the behavior from the human. It allows you to understand that due to a series of neurological responses and unconscious decisions you feel different feelings. Sometimes you feel anxious, sometimes you feel depressed, and sometimes you feel happy. Labeling yourself with your feelings and then allowing that label to dictate your life is simply an option.

Feelings are meant to be felt not worn as an identity. Think about it this way: Have you ever felt happy? If the answer is yes, have you then been diagnosed with happiness? No. What is the difference? You are not your feelings, and your feelings are not your identity. If a feeling feels like it's bigger than you and is overtaking your ability to process, get curious about which layer you are using to process it versus believing that the process will one day magically change. You are simply experiencing your feelings as your neurology was designed to do. I promise I will dive deeper into this later in this book, and it will make so much sense.

Start building a belief that feelings are temporary and are used as tools to show us how we respond to the world around us. They are not meant to be permanent identities. Your feelings and your experiences can greatly vary from the next person's. Imagine for a moment that you smell something amazing and try to explain the scent to your friend. The descriptive words you use to describe this "amazing" scent are pulled directly from your map as you attempt to explain what you've experienced. You may say it's woody or sweet or smells good. Your friend may trust you and take a whiff only to find out that it smells terrible. Your experience, your words, your values and your beliefs are completely different from what your friends experience.

You and your friend have unique responses because you have different maps. You may love onions for the taste while another person hates the smell of them. You may hate bananas because of their texture while your friend loves the flavor they provide. Think KAVOG. When you are experiencing these things, you are using completely different representational systems, values and beliefs to process how you experience the territory. This concept is laden in every single layer of your map. Understanding the meaning you give to things and the way they are encoded is an imperative part of editing your map. Trying to change people or fix people from your map is absolutely not sustainable and vice versa. Trying to edit your map while listening to someone else tell you where to make the edits is also not sustainable. Due to this being such a highly subjective space, I often share that the only form of help is self-help. Or as my friend John La Valle often shares, the person with the need is the one who has to do the work.[17]

Sustainable change comes from understanding the way you operate. It comes from understanding your map. It comes from knowing how you make decisions, what beliefs you hold around those spaces and what you value. There is no substitute for engaging with what's going on inside of you. Also, medicating these spaces does not bring sustainable change; it simply shuts down your ability to respond or care about how your physiology is experiencing them. It does not change the core challenge or belief that the challenge emanates from. Unfortunately, the world of Western psychology has not created access to this content or these strategies and instead continues to medicate these spaces. Knowing what you know now about your map and about NLP, how interested are you in learning how to heal these spaces from a holistic approach?

There is no substitute for engaging with what's going on inside of you.

Let's pause for a second. Allow me to create some awareness before we move on. I am absolutely not against medication as a temporary aid while you gain control, learn how to process trauma and get your feet back underneath you. However, using medication as a long-term tool to treat symptoms without ever exploring their roots does not move you forward. It simply creates a space where you can temporarily function. If the person writing these prescriptions is not *blatantly* explaining that to you, I would find someone you trust who can explain it in great detail. Your life is worthy of being lived fully, and quite possibly fully lived free from medication. If this idea challenges your thinking, please finish the book before negating it. There is much more in-depth information coming in future chapters.

Using different NLP models allows people to create absolute clarity in communication. Pulling your brain away from your map and allowing it to explore other parts of the territory is the ultimate goal, freeing it from any previous correlations or patterns. This freedom is beyond powerful when trying to edit and change your map. Remember that your beliefs, your values and your patterns all live on your map. When these are removed from your conscious processing, your ability to find new solutions and build new beliefs is endless.

How much sense is this starting to make? You now understand how you store information, how you process information and how you recall it. Now that we understand this foundational space, let's make a few connections. It was shared earlier that words provoke your neurology, and as you learned in this chapter, words are flexible. Every time you hear words, they bounce off your map and pull forward whatever meaning you previously assigned to them.

When people speak around you, you are constantly pulling forward *your* meaning and the story *you've* created around that word. When communication gets challenging, instead of being offended, hurt, intentionally wronged or left out, what might it feel like to instead believe *maybe our maps are just different* or *maybe my idea wasn't part of their map*? It also may empower you to ask yourself: What belief do I have that their presence is challenging? or What value of mind does this idea challenge? The challenge isn't that someone is right and someone is wrong. It's that you're communicating from two different maps and two different sets of values and beliefs.

Emotion comes when you feel like you're not being heard or when you feel like you're not being validated. Remember that words are anchored on your map in the emotion, the value and the belief that they were originally encoded in. The challenge lies in the map, not in the person or event that occurred. Creating awareness around your meaning, your history with that event and the map of the person speaking it now creates a wide space for new interpretation to occur.

The challenge lies in the map, not in the person or event that occurred.

Once you understand the story you are telling yourself and the power that story holds for you, you can then affect change. Take a moment and set this book down. Take a deep breath and relax. Take another deep breath and really consciously relax your entire body.

Now reflect back on the stories, the words or the thoughts that provoke you. Do they expand you or contract you? Where do you feel it in your body? What belief was that founded in? How does it now support or challenge your values?

Our physiology determines our psychology. Once we create awareness around how our story affects our neurology and how we have normalized it, we can take action and create sustainable change. What you collect on your map are all the ways that you have learned to speak, to lead, to think, to feel, to learn and to process. When your neurology operates at a faster pace than your conscious awareness, it makes complete sense that you continually repeat old unwanted patterns. Believing that there is a universal way of being and then experiencing quite the opposite in the real world would leave anyone confused. Learning that everyone is navigating their way through their life with their own personalized map allows you to release a bit of judgment and gain a bit more understanding of how this all works.

Direction is as valuable as destination. Once you create awareness around the patterns and the language you operate from, it allows you to understand this is simply who you have become and what it will take to get to the next step. Decide what direction you need to move in to accomplish your goals. Are you looking at the world as if it's a barricade that stops you from doing and living your dreams because it doesn't match your map of the world, or can you set your map down and look at the world as a series of opportunities you can grow through in order to accomplish your dreams?

Understanding the Narrative

Once you understand how you create success and how to use your words, you understand how to influence yourself and others. How do you know the things you know? How do you know the color yellow is actually yellow? And how do you discern between a dog barking in a cat meowing? How do you discern between a child calling out mom or dad and immediately knowing from the tone of their voice if they're in danger or if they just need you? You know all these things because they are encoded into your neurology through your representational systems, your five senses. You literally know what it *feels* like when your child cries out in pain versus what it *sounds* like. These are prime examples of healthy, effective unconscious responses. They have been anchored into your neurology and will lie dormant until they are awakened.

The other side of that question is: How many unhealthy, ineffective, unconscious responses do you have? Start identifying the words that immediately create a neurological response for you that keep you outside of success. Understand the origins of the word and how or why it plays a role in your life. Once you create awareness of the pattern that keeps you outside of your ideal outcome, it's really challenging to maintain that pattern. The more conscious energy you have around your patterns, the easier it is to find yourself in that ineffective loop pattern. Human neurology always accepts itself. It will always normalize a pattern even if it's completely ineffective or unhealthy. It will take your conscious awareness and create effective, sustainable change.

Understand your layers and what's on your map that's holding you outside of your ideal outcome. This can be done with a highly trained professional who understands the power of questions. The art of asking powerful questions and inviting self-discovery is the most effective route to change. When a coach or practitioner practices curiosity and asks you questions about your map, it keeps both parties out of judgment and inside the ability to stay curious.

As the questions come into your brain, your brain does a transderivational search through your map in an attempt to discover what is currently on your map, creating this challenge and hindering your access. A transderivational search is the act of locating information that may not be explicit on a surface, conscious level, allowing space for self-discovery. From that space, with further questioning, you also discover what changes need to happen in order to accomplish your goal. This is why telling people what to do and giving advice is not effective. People need to root through their own personal history and find out how that event established residency on their map. The easiest way through this journey is to be guided by powerful, intentional questions. For anyone who knows Dr. Bandler, one of his favorite words is *how*. The power the word *how* holds is incredible because it takes you directly into the belly of the challenge. The word *how* evokes awareness around the process you use to get to the next step. Learn *how* you get to the decisions, judgments and conclusions that rule your life.[18]

Powerful Questions

When you are working with the unconscious, the goal is to understand what the unconscious mind is doing process-wise. If your answer is repeatedly *I don't know*, that means it's out of your conscious awareness. The pattern is so deeply embedded in your unconscious mind that you are not even aware that you are running it. Start bringing your awareness to this process.

The words below are what I use as a trained professional when formulating questions for my clients. Much like pre-suppositions, each one of these words has its own ability to unpack certain spaces. When each word is paired with the content you are processing, it has the ability to reveal the action necessary for change.

How reveals PROCESS

What reveals CONTENT

When reveals TIME RECOGNITION

Who reveals RESOURCES

Where reveals LOCATION

Why reveals PURPOSE and often EMOTION

When used correctly, these five words can unveil deeply root-ed, unconscious information. If you are attempting a question with one of these words and either do not get an answer or get an unproductive response, ask the same question again using one of the other five words. For example, if you have a belief that emanates a highly emotional response, a trained professional might ask you one of these five questions:

- ➢ **How** do you know that that feeling goes with this scenario?
- ➢ **How** do you know when to start that feeling?
- ➢ **What** are you making this feeling mean?
- ➢ **When** was the first time you remember feeling this feeling?
- ➢ **Who** else was a part of this original feeling?
- ➢ **Where** do you feel this in your body?
- ➢ **Why** is this feeling important to you?

When you are attempting to create major sustainable change, like changing a belief, establishing a new belief system or unrooting something from your map, it takes a great deal of self-awareness and self-discovery. Both self-awareness and self-discovery are only possible by the person with the need. You cannot fix anyone because no one is broken. And you cannot change anyone. Changing people is not your job. Simply creating awareness and inviting self-discovery is what changes people. Map editing 101. Although this was a brief but impactful, one chapter overview of NLP, I know that it does not even scratch the surface; yet it's enough to create the foundational core necessary for understanding your map.

Questions for Insight

➢ What patterns have you identified that you were not previously aware of?

➢ How old were you the first time you ran each pattern?

➢ Where else in your life have you woven this pattern?

➢ How have you normalized this pattern and its presence?

_____

_____

_____

➢ What could you allow yourself to believe that releases this energy?

_____

_____

_____

➢ Why is that pattern of energy so powerful for you?

_____

_____

_____

➢ What is it about that story that you've allowed and normalized?

_____

_____

_____

Chapter 8

Spilling TEA

Your Emotional Foundation

Imagine that you are moving about your day, minding your own business, and out of nowhere this voice enters your physiology. It permeates your being, and you immediately feel hijacked. That voice enters your body on a cellular level, and it is not comfortable. Whether it's your partner's tone after a fight or a histrionic coworker's repetitive plea, your body responds before you are even aware. Said person's tone of voice is reverberating throughout your physiology and evoking a deep emotional response. You may think, *I just want them to stop talking*. Because of that thought and that emotional response you become frustrated, overwhelmed, distracted or simply unable to continue what you were doing until the noise ceases. You may be asking yourself how this happens.

All the information that you have read thus far leads you to understand that your neurology, your physiology and your psychology have been highly programmed, or patterned, to respond to the world around you, often in ways that are not always helpful or healthy. In this chapter we are going to un-pack and understand how behaviors are made, how we create behavior loops and how to interrupt those spaces to invite change. We will also dive deeper into thoughts, emotions and behaviors and learn how they connect to your beliefs and how those layers all relate to your map. This chapter is what I refer to as spilling TEA.

TEA is an acronym for thought, emotion, action (action, outcome or behavior). Every response starts with TEA; a thought creates an emotion, and then that powerful combo results in an action, outcome or behavior. The question becomes what emotions and actions your thoughts are creating for you. Spilling TEA, a US slang term, is often used when people are gossiping about other people and sharing their business without their permission. I think it's an incredibly powerful analogy here and used in the same context. Unbeknownst to you, your behavior is always telling on you. It's always spilling your TEA. Your behavior is a direct result of the emotions and thoughts you are processing. So, without your knowledge, you as well spill TEA all day, every day to all the people around you. Understanding that space and learning about your TEA and the reality it creates for you is fundamental in acquiring sustainable change.

Here's where things start to get a bit interesting. You have embraced the idea that everyone was born with a blank map; and you now understand that you have spent the duration of your life building and collecting each layer of your own, subjective map at a highly unconscious level. Now you can start learning, identifying and dismantling the behaviors that emanate from it. Remember that we don't know what we don't know, and change begins with awareness. Changing behaviors first starts with knowing how they are created. It starts with learning how behaviors are made, understanding the different pieces of behaviors, how they work and what engages them. Each one of these fundamental pieces is layered into your map.

Because your brain is consistently working towards efficiency, over time your patterns become looped and run unconsciously with little guidance or input from you. Some of this may sound very familiar, as the majority of it was covered in the previous chapters, yet this is the point in the process where we start engaging with each layer as we attempt to affect change. Learning, understanding, and then identifying the function of each piece of your behavior patterns, what each piece does and how those pieces are built is incredibly imperative in affecting change.

Although this may sound very abstract right now, it's actually very simple. Over time, you have normalized your patterns because they are continually running on a loop, without any conscious awareness. Think about it like this, remember the first time you learned how to drive a car? My guess is that you had to orient yourself in the driver's seat, find the seatbelt, secure it in place, adjust the seat so that your feet could reach the pedals and make sure your hands were at ten and two. Then you had to adjust your mirrors to make sure they reflected what was outside of the car so you could keep those things in your vision while managing what's happening inside the car and on the road. All these adjustments had to be pretty accurate for you to find success as a driver. And that's before you even started the car! Once you started the car you had to pace your speed, acknowledge the other drivers around you, stay in your lane, accurately stop at lights leaving space between you and the car in front of you, and consistently maintain each one of these things the entire time you are driving.

I'm not sure about you, but I'm kind of embarrassed to admit how many things I'm capable of doing now while driving a car. My guess is that I'm not alone in this. Currently driving, I can hold or reach for my water bottle, adjust the climate controls, find a new podcast episode, start or stop a new call (or God forbid a Zoom call if necessary—let's be honest, it happens), shift the air circulation, find my ChapStick, dig for a piece of gum, possibly even yell at my daughter in the back seat because she's distracting me, all while driving 60 miles an hour down the road. The reason we can do all these things is because we are unconsciously competent and are running in default mode.

This is the same for you. You have unconsciously programmed your brain to understand what to watch for outside of your car. You have created this internal and external cadence, and your physiology is hardwired to pick up any nuances that are out of the norm. You are moving about with minimal conscious awareness. Yet in the event of a change, your neurology would immediately see red brake lights or a person or animal on the side of the road or God forbid even a ball rolling directly in front of your car. Your physiology would respond well before you would. It's events like these that instantly awaken your neurology and your physiology and snap you into conscious awareness.

Your brain is doing this same thing throughout your entire day. It is seeking the path to efficiency, the shortest route with minimal effort, in hopes of preserving and protecting your energy. You have normalized how your different patterns feel and you give them zero conscious awareness until you are called to do so. Once you are asked to place conscious awareness on those areas, things get a bit harder. Things require actual effort. That's why it may feel overwhelming to comprehend learning new things. You are super used to things being easy.

Imagine how challenging it would have been to learn to drive while holding a water bottle, listening to a podcast, putting on ChapStick, being on a Zoom call and having kids in the backseat talking to you. It would have been extremely overwhelming! Yet that's not how you or I learned. We learned to add things in slowly; as we normalized the actions over time, and we became unconsciously competent, so we then added in more.

This layered content of TEA is much the same. You continually layer in new content on top of old patterns. This will make more sense as you begin reflecting, catching yourself in motion and acknowledging how your neurology, physiology and psychology respond. Understanding how behaviors are made is one of the most fundamental pieces of affecting change in human behavior. How many of these sound familiar to you?

- ➤ He always makes me so mad.
- ➤ My boss annoys me.
- ➤ Their behavior frustrates me.
- ➤ Her words hurt my feelings.
- ➤ My kids are pushing all my buttons.

And how often do you hear this same pattern that something externally caused an internal response for you? This belief alludes to the idea that the external world is responsible for your internal world. *Nothing could be further from the truth.* This chapter is about learning that behaviors are actually the end result of a chain reaction. They are the external action/ behavior/reaction to your internal processing.

Now that you have uncovered how your brain works, my guess is that you have started to uncover things on your map that both positively and negatively affect your life. With this new awareness, what's coming up for you? What are the behaviors, responses or reactions that are standing out that you'd like to adjust, remove or edit?

Take a moment and write down all the things that are coming up for you. Write down what behaviors you'd like to change. Write down what you believe is stopping you or interrupting your access to your success. If you need to word that question differently, please feel free to do so. The goal here is to write down all the things that you would edit, if you only had access.

➢ What are your biggest challenges?

➢ What behavior keeps repeating itself and hinders your growth?

➤ What frustrates you the most?

➤ What thoughts continually run that you would like to change, shift or edit?

➤ What behavior or outcome repeats itself consistently that creates a barrier to your success?

Share in as much detail as possible what it is that's holding you back from your goals. This is a very important step. The more content you write down, the more access you will find to you.

_____

_____

_____

_____

_____

_____

Thank you, friend. Take a moment and thank yourself too. Learning how to change is one thing. Opening up, getting vulnerable and doing the work is a completely different story. Allow yourself to stand in that for a moment and begin to normalize what it feels like to take the time, to honor yourself and to heal. Normalize healing. Namaste, friend.

Although changing behaviors does create change, there is so much more to it than that. It's possible you experience a behavior and then decide that's not the behavior you want, so you attempt to change what occurred in your external world, expecting sustainable results internally. You may respond by saying something like *don't talk to me like that* or *don't act like that* or *stop pushing my buttons* because their response does not match your map of the world *and* their words are triggering something deep inside you. Triggers are intense, especially if they catch you off guard. Triggers are an emotional reaction that is often larger than the initial emotion that created it. They lead to uncontrollable emotions and often come as a result of unprocessed trauma. Knowing all of that, allow yourself some time and space to learn more about what triggers you and unpack the origins of your triggers. Leading further into the idea that what you experience externally either finds alignment or feels out of alignment with what's going on internally, know how these things are attached to your layered map.

How Behaviors Are Made

Looking back at the stuff you have written down, let's jump into the TEA model as promised. This is one of the most effective coaching models I have found to date, and it also comprises your last three layers. The TEA model is a three-step process that builds awareness using a high-level approach to disassemble how behaviors are made. The TEA model is based on the foundation that behaviors are the result of the emotion and the thought(s) that precede them.

Simplified: Thoughts create emotions, and emotions then create actions, outcomes and behaviors. That's it. That's the whole thing.

I know what you're thinking! It sounds so simple. How in the hell could it be this easy? Stay with me. Oftentimes you attempt to change the behavior because that's what stands out to you as being ineffective or unpleasant, yet the behavior is the end result of a chain reaction. In order to change a behavior, you actually have to reverse engineer the process and unpack what started the rolling trickle-down effect. Take a moment and observe the graphic on the next page.

internal processing

TEA Model
coaching model

internal states

internal or external
KAVOG

action
external response
behaviors • outcome

©2022 by Jodee Gibson

As you can see, actions emanate from emotions, and emotions are created by thoughts. Thoughts evoke from an internal or external KAVOG trigger—you feel something, you hear something, you see something, you smell something or you taste something—that is attached to an old story and engages your map. The first step that initiates a behavior is the trigger. How you decide to respond to that trigger is completely up to you. When your phone rings, do you get frustrated? Do you get excited? Do you answer your phone even if you are mid-conversation with a different person, creating a socially awkward moment, and then blame your phone for ringing? How do you respond in these moments? Understanding your responses to the consistent barrage of triggers is the beginning of creating effective sustainable change.

Think about it like this: your phone rings, you glance at it, you read the name, make a decision and then take action. Or maybe your stomach growls and you realize you're hungry. You reflect back to the last time you've eaten or maybe check your watch for the time, creating awareness around if it is or is not lunch time. With that information, you decide if you are going to tend to the hunger pains or keep pushing through without eating.

External Trigger→	Thought→	Emotion→	Action/Behavior
Phone rings	It's my friend	Excitement	Answer the phone
Phone rings again	It's my boss	Annoyed	Ditch to voicemail
		...feeling overwhelmed...	
			...yelling at the kids
Internal Trigger→	**Thought→**	**Emotion→**	**Action/Behavior**
Stomach growls	What time is it?	Perseverance	Keep working
	I'm hungry...		
		...feeling insecure...	

For the rows with the light grey, try filling in the blanks. What comes after these thoughts, or what thoughts and emotions build the examples shown here?

Remember that your brain is constantly seeking two things: belonging and efficiency. Because your brain is consistently working toward efficiency, its goal is to close the perceived gap as quickly as possible. Your phone rings, your brain wants your phone to stop ringing. Your stomach growls, your brain either obliges or ignores. Your muscles ache, you either stop or push through. Your feelings come up, you either acknowl-edge them or push them down. Your kids yell your name four thousand times a day, you tune them out or take action if they truly need you. The point here is to understand that these consistent responses become normalized over time. Because your brain is seeking efficiency, it builds an unconscious re-sponse pattern. We normalize our actions, outcomes and behaviors. Because of this consistency, the repeated pattern eventually creates a loop (more on that later).

These are the patterns, loops and behaviors that build your map. It's these spaces that evoke comments like *that's just who I am* or *that's the way we do it* without ever investigat-ing the history of the pattern. How much more clarity does it create to say *this is who I've become over time* or *this is the way we have unconsciously been doing it for years*, embracing the conscious awareness of how that pattern of behavior was built? These anchored patterns, loops and behaviors on your map are the exact things that stay in the way of your success, because this is the map you are unknowingly using to navi-gate the territory. Knowing that, the majority of the content collected on your map lies dormant until it's triggered, either internally or externally. Things can lie dormant for decades and only come to the surface when the same KAVOG trig-ger appears.

What the TEA model so clearly teaches is that when your brain is triggered, internally or externally, you internally pro-cess what you just observed. So, your brain does a transderi-vational search throughout your entire map, finds something similar to what it's experiencing and then creates a thought. That thought then searches again throughout your map through all your memories, including any previously dropped anchors, seeks out similar things and then attaches an emo-tion to what it processed. From that emotional response, an action is created—a behavior. That behavior is a result of everything that came before it.

Changing a behavior without investigating its roots is like trying to change a maple tree into a lemon tree. Imagine that a whirlybird seed from a maple tree falls and is planted in a random spot. The rain, the sunshine and the climate around it allows it to grow uninterrupted. Almost overnight the seed sprouts and a tree is born, and within a few years the tree is strong with sturdy roots, ready for future growth. Expecting that tree to now bear lemons sounds ludicrous, huh? That's the same idea as expecting a different behavior from the same TEA.

Know this: you could absolutely tape lemons all over that maple tree and say I'm getting lemons and can create lemonade from this tree. Yet how long would it take before the tape became gooey and the fruit fell to the ground? At that point the fruit-bearing aspect simply becomes ineffective. This is the same exact thing as trying to change a behavior. You have to investigate the roots, the layers of the action, before you can expect sustainable change. Treating the symptom—we need lemons—but never realizing that you're seeking lemons from a maple tree is a prime example of ignoring the root cause. Let's explore a few additional examples to solidify the theory.

External Trigger

Imagine you are driving down the freeway, and you see a car that's driving recklessly (external trigger). You might immediately think *that driver doesn't look safe*, or *that driver has been drinking*, or *that driver is impaired*, or *that driver needs help* (thought). Whatever thought comes through to you, it then provokes an emotion. The emotional response could be fear, worry, danger, anxiety or a myriad of other emotions that match that experience (emotion). Then from that emotion comes your response, your action. You choose to either retreat and exit the freeway or pass the car in hopes of getting ahead of any possible crash, call the police and alert them, or drive up next to the car and engage with the driver (action/behavior). Whichever of these you choose to do is dependent upon the thought that initially grew from the trigger you experienced and the emotional decision that followed. Saying something like *that driver made me leave the freeway* is not actually correct. Breaking it down into the *T*, *E*, and *A* steps allows you to see there were multiple choices involved. This combo built the behavior you experienced.

Internal Trigger

Imagine that we meet as friends, and you share that you are afraid of dogs. Maybe this is because as a very small child you were approached by a dog and that dog startled you. He may have nipped at you, sniffed at your face or touched you with his wet nose, and it scared the holy life out of you (thought). This memory was anchored on your map with intense emotion when you were maybe three years old. In the present day, maybe you are forty-five or fifty years old, which means you've practiced this *I'm afraid of dogs* (thought—your theory) response for more than forty years. Each time you see a dog (the sight of the dog is an internal trigger that engages your theory), what it pulls forward is sheer terror (emotion). Even if you've only encountered a dog two or three times a year for the past forty-plus years, that means you have practiced this response over one hundred times. Each time you see a dog now, it instantaneously comes flooding back, and that moment is relived. The movie replays in your head, and you become terrified with the mere thought of it. Remember that we recall memories in pictures, and the more times we recall the pictures, those pictures eventually turn into videos. You now have an emotionally intense experience from the mere sight of a dog (action/behavior).

The art of learning about triggers is understanding which are useful and which are not and then learning how to think on purpose. What do you want to feel? How do you create that feeling? And what do you need to think about in order to get there? I invite you to sit down with your dog engagement memory, or your I'm afraid of water story, your I'm afraid of elevators or spiders story, your I'm bad at math story, or any other story you have created in your mind. Sit down and unpack the TEA. Walk yourself through each piece of the loop and identify the validity of its counterparts. Identify each step, each piece, and get in the weeds with your insight. Become aware of the stories you are telling yourself and unpack those spaces like never before.

Reflect on the things you jotted down in the beginning of this chapter.

➢ What did you share as your biggest challenges?

_____

_____

_____

➢ What is the behavior that keeps repeating itself, hindering your growth?

➢ What is it that frustrates you the most?

➢ What thoughts continually run that you would like to change, shift or edit?

➢ What behavior or outcome continues to repeat itself consistently that creates a barrier to your success?

Take a moment and get a bit deeper with your answers. Use the chart below to navigate through your answers. If you have listed a behavior, reverse engineer it and find the emotions that drive it. Then find the thought that created that emotional response. Lastly, unpack what it is that triggers that thought. Do this for each of your answers. Work in either direction or start in whichever column you have answers for. Also know that this is a work in progress. Know that more answers will come as more content is revealed in the following chapters. If you get stuck on one, that's ok. The balance of the answers will reveal themselves over time and with conscious awareness.

Also note, you have consistently normalized each and every piece of this step-by-step process. Things may not stand out to you, and you may have to dig for them or allow them to reveal themselves the next time that pattern runs for you. What you are looking for is the emotional/energetic pattern that is engaged by a trigger.

Trigger	Thought	Emotion	Action/Behavior
You wake up late for work.	I'm going to get fired. I'm going to lose my job.	Frustrated. Disappointed.	Pissed off that my whole day is ruined and maybe my whole life.

How powerful is it to now understand what's driving your actions/behaviors? Once you have conscious awareness of how and why you do the things you do, you then have the necessary access to change things. Awareness creates access. The more awareness you create, the more patterns you will find. You will begin to see the patterns in your behavior that are linked together. You will identify some of your core beliefs and the foundations they create for you. Through this process you will uncover limiting beliefs—*I should put their needs first*, *my voice doesn't matter*, *I'm not smart*, *I'm bad at math*, etc. You may also uncover assumptions like *it doesn't really matter*, *my opinion doesn't count*, or *they won't care anyway*. Use the TEA model and allow yourself to uncover these common thoughts and find your foundational beliefs on your map. Remember that your beliefs are your version of the world, and they create your map. Understanding their function and their source is imperative to your personal growth.

The majority of your TEA responses are built from old beliefs, old layers that no longer serve you; and up until this moment, you probably had zero awareness of them. It's the same as saying things like *dogs are scary*. That statement makes total sense to you because the today version of you is trying to process the presence of a dog with a paralyzed, terrified three-year-old's emotion. This is how limiting beliefs are born. Old thought + new goal = limited perspective. Keep using this tool and keep creating awareness. Like anything else, the more you practice, the more awareness and access you will have. Remember, we can only change the things we are aware of.

Know too that it's completely normal if this was a struggle for you, or if it didn't evoke a huge awareness. Because you have normalized most of these patterns, they may not stand out to you at first. You may believe this whole chapter is frustrating. As time passes and you find yourself in that space again, this step-by-step process will stand out; something will click, and you will have an aha moment. Know that there is a grand difference between skimming the surface (snorkeling) and getting deep to the root of the weeds (scuba diving). In order to affect change, you are going to have to scuba dive.

From that journey you will have new awareness around your patterns and your roots. Know that it's ok for this process to take time. Surface isn't where change happens. Surface is where you hide stuff, where you camouflage what's really happening. The surface level produces symptoms that emanate from the underlying root. That root permeates every part of your map. In order to uncover layers, you have to identify the root system. Work backwards if needed. Reverse engineer it. The weeds are at the bottom, in the trenches, and I promise you they are easier to find with the TEA method than any other method I've found to date. The roots represent an underlying value or belief. Until you identify the root of your symptoms, the symptoms will persist. Think about how many years you have already spent normalizing and soothing symptoms. Take the time and allow that space to heal. Once healed, what grows from that space is healthy, productive intentional thoughts. Taking time to unpack it is healthy. Remember, slow and steady wins the race.

Rebuilding Emotions

The way in which an emotion enters your body is the way in which you will forever recall it, if and until you intentionally change it. HARD STOP. You will forever store emotions on your map in the way in which you learned them until you learn differently. Your thoughts invite and evoke emotional responses.

Although some of these responses may often feel like they come out of nowhere, know that they are being pulled directly off of your map. And, your emotions are tied directly to your boundaries, your expectations and your awareness. The more fluent you become in each and every one of these layers, the more access you have to mastering your emotions. As you begin to master this space, you will uncover the notion that your emotions are 100 percent a decision (consciously or unconsciously). And depending upon how deeply looped your responses are, your awareness around your decisions was probably not even evident until now.

Your Emotions Are Your Decision

Although you may or may not agree with that statement, by the end of this chapter, you will be super fluent in that truth. Your behavior emerges from your emotional responses. This response is 100 percent dependent upon the story and the thought that created it. It is a direct result of the powerful combo that built it. What keeps these behaviors cycling and eventually loops them is confirmation bias. Adding one more layer on, once action/behavior is created and emerges, you will seek out things in the world to confirm that you are right and have made the right decision. This is called confirmation bias.

Confirmation bias is when you find things in the world that support your map, your perspective and your action. Confirmation bias allows you to believe that you made the right choice and that there is evidence of that all around you. Confirming your thoughts, acknowledging your actions and feeling validated about them is a normal process. This is how loops are created. As a mastery level coach, my expertise lies in this space, understanding loops and unpacking human behavior.

thought
internal processing

TEA Loops™
coaching model

emotion
internal states
anchors • memories

action
external response
behaviors • outcome

confirmation bias
replaces trigger
external matches experience

©2022 by Jodee Gibson

TEA Loops™

Now that you have learned how behaviors are made and how the TEA model works, let's explore how loops work and how they impact your life. What happens in the TEA model (as well as in the Six Layers of Human Behavior) is what you now know is a four-step process. There is a trigger (internal or external) that provokes a thought. The thought engages an emotion, which creates an action/behavior. Once the behavior emerges, you unconsciously seek out confirmation that you have made the correct choice. In a loop, the trigger is replaced with confirmation bias. Behaviors reinforce beliefs. The more you run this pattern it eventually becomes a looped response and runs on default. You learned previously about neuroplasticity and the bike path; these are the same. Your brain seeks out a familiar path and off it goes. *See TEA loop model.*

Changing this loop requires trust and vulnerability. Loops are based on beliefs. The easiest way to unpack a loop is to identify the founding belief and then age that belief. How old were you the first time you remember running this loop? How did this looped response serve you then? How does it serve you now? What is the founding belief that keeps the loop running today? Where else in your life does this pattern show up? If you were eight years old the first time you ran this loop, and it's that same belief that's running it today, my question is where else in your life are you allowing an eight-year-old to make decisions for you. Remember, the belief is anchored in your then aged emotional comprehension (more on this in chapter 13). If you were eight years old when this loop was built, your emotional capacity to run this loop is founded in an eight-year-old's understanding of the concept and will continually run at this eight-year-old capacity until it's unpacked. Even more interesting, you have completely normalized this process.

The more a loop is repeated, it will eventually build a powerful belief. The more you repeated the old stories and recycled the old emotions, the more you looped things together that were not related, yet it made sense as a child to connect those emotional responses. Also, the more things you have linked together, the more impactful and heavier the loop can feel. Imagine that as a child you often got picked last for the team in gym class. This happened not for any other reason than that's simply how the cards fell. Over time, you may begin to have an emotional response and may feel a bit abandoned or left out, as if the action was intentional. Because this emotional response intensified each time this occurred, you built a powerful belief around it, and it has been anchored on your map. We discussed the psychological sunburn in a previous chapter. Now, when someone doesn't invite you to a party or include you in weekend plans, that previous experience, that psychological sunburn, feels so intense and nearly explosive when it occurs now. This intensity comes because you've been unconsciously practicing it for years.

The only way to heal a loop is to open it up and release the energy that keeps it cycling (more on energy in chapter 9). This can be done in multiple ways. Because loops have several pieces to them, catching yourself in any of those spaces and not completing the action leaves the loop open, inviting space to create conscious awareness, to make a different decision and to begin to heal.

Regardless of where you find yourself in the loop, the entire goal is to stop the loop from closing. If the loop stays open, it provides you an opportunity to unpack the story and not validate it, even if you have already been triggered. Taking intentional action right in that moment and stopping the loop from closing, or the event from finishing, is imperative. It would be like watching the whirlybird fall from the maple tree, seed itself, open and sprout yet right before it starts growing you step in and pull the roots out, stopping it from any future growth. This is how you change a loop. Intentionally and with great purpose.

You can do this same thing by stepping back and gaining conscious awareness of what triggers your pattern and then interrupting the patterns once you find yourself in them. The more awareness you have around each piece of a loop, the more control you gain. Remember, we can only change what we acknowledge. The more the loop stays open, the easier it becomes to create a new, healthy, intentional loop. This is neuroplasticity at its finest.

When our loop is open, we are vulnerable and highly suggestive. This is where beliefs are born. It's how the loop was built in the first place. You trusted someone or something and unknowingly allowed yourself to build a belief and housed it on your map. That same process requires your conscious trust and vulnerability now. Remember from earlier that the way in which an emotion enters your body is the way in which it will be recalled. The same applies in your loops. Whatever input goes in when the loop is open, eventually gets locked in, looped in, and the loop runs until you interrupt it.

People often want to experience a different emotion or behavior, yet they're not aware of the TEA process or the origins of their map. Once you have awareness of where your thoughts emanate from, the source of your emotions, the foundation of your actions, and what validation or confirmation you are seeking, you are then able to navigate intentionally. Until all four of those things are in concert, you are simply living in a default state, trying to see new parts of the territory while navigating around with an old, outdated map. Change requires vulnerability. Vulnerability improves deep human connections. Once you are ready to get vulnerable, you are ready to grow. Once you have awareness of what thoughts you are generating and what emotions they are connected to, you can start generating new loops. Expecting to immediately be fixed isn't realistic, yet know that each time you interrupt the pattern, you stop the loop from closing. That action in itself begins paving a new road to sustainable change, again and again and again.

It all begins with conscious awareness and intentional thinking. One of the things Dr. Bandler consistently shares is the power that comes from thinking versus remembering.

Learn to think on purpose. Learn to think about what is actually possible versus remembering what happened last time. Thinking and remembering are two completely different activities. Remembering your way through life will not give you more access to the territory.[19]

Creating new beliefs as we grow is how we create the life we want. Get vulnerable. Recognize that you may have blind spots. Trust yourself and learn to trust the process. Free yourself from the old, outdated layers of you and step into what's possible. Know that when you feel stuck in life, odds are high it's an old belief versus an actual obstacle. If you feel stuck, know that you are simply remembering and engaging an outdated layer that does not have the capacity to process what you are asking. Think intentionally. Unpack the TEA. It is absolutely okay and incredibly healthy to stumble your way through this. It's all normal in personal growth. Also, know that overwhelm comes when we are attached to the outcome or have a huge expectation instead of being present in the moment. Learn to be present. Be open to new thinking.

As shared earlier, unpacking human behavior is my fluent language. The TEA tool makes that process so much easier; and I believe, once you learn and integrate it, it too will become an easy practice for you. Know that your brain is like a computer, your unconscious mind always responds first and reverts to the original meaning that you encoded that memory in, whether that's a word, an emotion, a feeling, a sound or an energy. Know that that voice, that song, that feeling or whatever that trigger resurfaces is simply an old, outdated layer. In much the same way, if I ask you what letter comes after *k*, odds are high you would sing the alphabet song, waiting for what comes after *k*. You're singing the alphabet song because that's how you learned the alphabet. What else in your life is that predictable?

Questions for Insight

➢ What triggers, emotions, behaviors or loops have you identified that consistently show up in your world?

➢ What emotions frequently surface because they are unknowingly triggered without your consent or desire?

➢ What emotions, behaviors or loops might you be ignoring or not believing are actually playing a role in your output?

➤ What patterns keep repeating themselves, even if they are in different areas of your life, especially the uninvited ones?

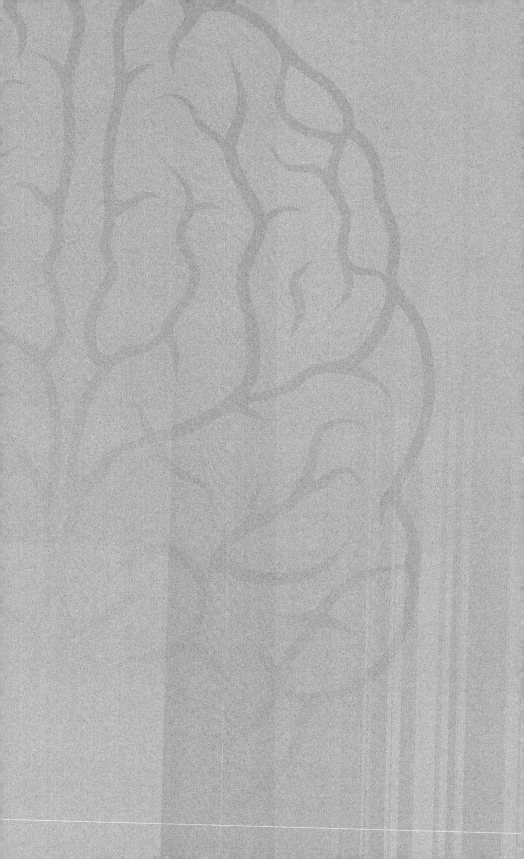

Chapter 9

Understanding Consciousness— Expand and Contract

W hat keeps people outside of their goals or their ideal performance is rarely skill level. It's almost always their thoughts and the level of energy (LOE) with which they approach them. I cannot place enough attention on the importance of learning and understanding the law of vibration. This is the same exact content Napoleon Hill shared in 1937 and Dr. David Hawkins shared in 1987, yet people are still negating it.

The topography of your map lies
in the law of vibration.

Each person, place, and thing has a frequency at which it vibrates, and that frequency becomes its default LOE. Energy in this case has a specific meaning. There's likely been a time when you were moving about your day, minding your own business, and you suddenly feel through every cell in your being that someone is watching you, only to look up and lock eyes with that person. That's energy. Or maybe there was a time when you knew someone had arrived at your house, not because of a visual or auditory clue, but more because you felt the energy shift with their presence. That's energy. It's what you call a coincidence when you think of a person just before they call you, or when you remember your favorite song right before it plays on the radio.

There may have been a time when you entered a house and immediately started looking for the exit because the energy just felt off and you wanted out. Or quite the opposite, when you arrived at someone's home and instantly felt the soothing, cathartic energy of peace, warmth, and connection welcoming you in. The energy was so inviting you wanted to stay as long as possible, absorbing it just a bit more. Each one of those examples is evidence that energy is all around you. The question becomes are you expanded enough to feel these moments, or might you be so contracted that they do not even hit your radar.

Know this: Everything is energy. *Everything*.

Understanding the law of vibration is of utmost importance as it allows you to recognize how each and every piece of your map was built and what LOE each one of your layers have been anchored in. The law of vibration is remarkably stronger and more powerful than the law of attraction. It is also testable and measurable. Dr. David Hawkins, the creator of the often referred to Map of Consciousness™, proved this theory with muscle testing. Every single thing around you carries a frequency that your body detects. Everything. Negating this fact has the capacity to put you lightyears behind your goals. Learning and embracing this law has the capacity to change the trajectory of your life. Know what your default LOE is and what it attracts to you.[20]

Intentional Consciousness™

Remember that the map you started with was blank. This next chapter will help you uncover what LOE each piece of your map has been encoded in and how that plays a role with the TEA you build. This level of Intentional Consciousness allows you to manifest your life like never before.

Imagine standing on the patio of the most incredible mountainside house you have ever experienced. The sprawling patio is connected to a breathtaking wrap-around porch that travels around the entire exterior circumference of the house. As you walk the path, the 360-degree view overtakes all of your senses as you take in the most incredulous skyline. You can smell the salt coming off the ocean. The sea of blinking lights leaves you in utter wonder of exactly what awaits when the early sunlight drenches the overlooking city. The energy feels alive yet calm as the soothing night air brushes your skin. Regardless of the time of day, your view has endless beauty to take in, and you allow your imagination to run wild. The views are free from interruption and create a weightless, surreal, possible, infinite, and present feeling throughout.

Yesterday does not exist. Tomorrow is way too far away. You are here now, and it feels like magic.

In an instant your feet slide back about three feet, and a door slams shut in front of you, blocking your entire view. The only remnant left of what you know to be is on the other side of this gigantic, structurally sound, larger than life set of doors. That wide open space of wonder has just been compacted into this little, tiny peephole in the door that just slammed your dreams shut. All of them. Paralyzed. Speechless. Frozen in time, you keep looking through this tiny peephole in the door, embracing what's left of that glorious moment yet nothing compares. You feel trapped. Contracted. Unable to imagine.

One thing I know for sure is everything in life either makes you expand or contract. You've seen me share this same idea repeatedly throughout the book, yet you may not have known exactly what it meant. Let me be really clear: This is the part of the story that no one is talking about; or maybe I should say only a few people are talking about it, but no one is listening.

This is the part that changes everything.

This is the pivotal content.

This is the missing piece that people stumble past yet continue to search for. They talk around it and they reference it, yet very few people actually know how it works. This is the research-based, scientifically proven content that is as certain as the laws of gravity. When I say that everything in life makes you expand or contract, the idea I'm conveying is that each one of our life experiences includes a physiological response, an internal cue, that alerts us and affects each one of us in totally different ways. This physiological response has been so utterly normalized overtime to the point that you don't even realize it's happening. These physiological responses invade every single layer of your being and are highly trained and heavily patterned. Your physiology and your neurology respond in ways you have never realized you had control over. The state of your physiology determines the experience you have.

Think back to our patio scenario. How different were the feelings you experienced? Standing on the edge of glory, fully embodying the idea that you are invincible compared to standing completely opposite of everything you have ever wanted, knowing it's within reach yet barricaded by what feels like a gigantic, immovable door.

Whether it's Napoleon Hill's theory behind *Think and Grow Rich* or Dr. David Hawkins's evidence behind the *Map of Consciousness*, this concept is not new, it's just often misunderstood. What I will share with you in the next chapter is an incredibly layered approach to the culmination of both of their work, including Bruce D Schneider's work, the content I received in my coaches training, Esther Hicks's work, Abraham Hicks's work, Dr. Wayne Dyer and Dr. Richard Bandler's genius theories, and a few others. The principles underlying this work has been referred to as the Map of Consciousness, the laws of attraction, the scales of vibration, the law of vibration, quantum physics and many other things. Instead of inventing and adding another term, I will refer to it as the law of vibration, which houses the levels of energy (LOE). The entire goal is to teach you about the presence of anabolic and catabolic energy that exist inside those theories, as well as inside of you.[21]

Shifting Energy

If you're trying to shift into an expanded energy, know that it takes intentional practice. Every time you retell an old story, you're telling the universe more of this please, and it finds similar scenarios for you to re-experience that LOE. You watch crime shows because your brain is addicted to the catabolic burst of energy, as it's that exact familiar energy that soothes your nervous system. Your brain has been trained to seek out trauma and then soothe it with the story of survival. Knowing that emotion is simply energy in motion, your neurology has been conditioned and trained to seek out and find the exact LOE that it was originally encoded in. With that being your default, your layered map vibrates at the capacity that you do. It attracts to it the same energy it emits.

Again, much like water, energy self-levels. The seven levels of energy that we will dive into in this chapter are the topography of your map. Know that it makes complete sense if this feels a little woo-woo right now, yet remember that Napoleon Hill[22] started this conversation in 1937, and Dr. David Hawkins dug even deeper in 1987. I continue to share those dates with you because this content is well over a hundred years old, yet only a handful of people completely understand it and use it intentionally. This research-based, scientifically proven content is far from woo-woo.

Your vibration, your frequency, your emotion and your default LOE are all directly related to the reality you have and will continue to experience on a daily basis. This is the energy we refer to when we say emotion is simply energy in motion. This is why some emotions feel so heavy and nearly paralyzing for you, while others feel so light and free. You can have all the intention in the world yet be unable to access your ideal outcome because the LOE you are unconsciously vibrating at does not align with the outcome you are seeking. Creating utter awareness around your default LOE and understanding what it pulls forward is imperative for you to reach the level of success you desire.

You cannot get an expanded outcome from a contracted equation. HARD STOP. Thriving outcomes are not built in victim mode. Anabolic energy causes your physiology to expand and open. Catabolic energy causes it to contract and close.

Like energies attract like energies. Just like two magnets, like energies attract like opportunities, like outcomes, like relationships, like environments, like cultures and so much more. As we discussed with the TEA process, the only way to change the outcome you are experiencing is to become self-aware of which LOE has created it. The most ideal way is with conscious awareness and intentional action. Remember that energy is much like water. How much sense would it make right now if I told you I want to take a bath, yet I only want to put water in the back of the bathtub, not in the front. It's not possible, is it? It's not possible because that's not how it works. Water self-levels, and so does energy! It may sound redundant, but the default LOE at which you vibrate is what creates the territory you experience. When your map has deep emotions (energy) anchored in different layers, it often feels impossible to change, shift or experience anything other than where you are *stuck*.

Levels of Energy

Depending on whose theory you study, there are roughly seven levels of energy that encompass all the emotions we experience. In this chapter, I will share the seven levels of energy, explain the differences in each one, reveal what each one pulls forward and explain how they are all connected. It's common for people to jump into this chapter and want to choose one level that represents them because that's the level that makes them feel good. However, much like the idea that you are not the label of your feelings, you are not the LOE you are experiencing. You are simply experiencing that energy. I often hear people say, "I am a level six" or "I am a level one when I'm mad." You are not a LOE. You are simply experiencing level six energy or experiencing level one energy. Much like your feelings are not your identity, your energy is also not your identity. Although we all have an ideal LOE, rarely is that our default LOE. As you read through the different levels, know that you experience all of them at some point.[23]

Allow yourself to understand and embrace the idea that everyone bounces up and down, back and forth, through all seven levels all day long. There is no one person on the planet that continually stays in one level. Although we do have a dominant level, we have fluidity in the space in which we process information. This chapter also shares the theory behind anabolic and catabolic energy and the differences between them. Often people lean into the idea that anabolic energy is good and catabolic is the opposite. That is far from the truth. Like yin and yang, the up needs a down and the in needs an out. Anabolic energy would not be nearly as powerful if catabolic energy did not exist. Neither is good or bad. We need both energies to function.

Anabolic energy, as explained by Dr. Hawkins, is constructive and life-enhancing. Anabolic energy is what makes you expand. It creates your internal freedom. It is the feeling that arrived when you step onto the patio and feel like the world is yours. It's the feeling you get when you see your child for the first time—or any time for that matter. It's the feeling that overtakes your neurology when you see the person you love and everything about you simply feels aligned. It's the feeling of pure and utter freedom that you experience in numerous activities you joyfully find yourself in. It's weightless, endless and holds no barriers. The higher the level of anabolic energy present, the more you feel is possible. Anabolic energy is incredibly addictive due to the natural high you experience when you experience it. When anabolic energy is present, your body sets off endorphins and your brain is saturated with happy chemicals. It allows you to create, dream, imagine, release, and expand. The higher your LOE, the more anabolic energy will be present.[24]

As Dr. Hawkins shares, catabolic energy is quite the opposite. Catabolic energy is destructive. It's paralyzing and life-consuming. The caveat to catabolic energy is understanding when it's present and how to intentionally leverage it. Without your conscious awareness, catabolic energy can wreak havoc on your life. Catabolic energy engages your fight or flight mode. Catabolic energy is the feeling you get when you are home alone and hear a strange noise that is completely out of the norm. A fire hose fills your body with adrenaline. Every hair on the back of your neck stands on end, and your feet feel as though you could run a mile, yet you are utterly frozen, left wearing cement shoes. It's the feeling you get when you're caught off guard by another's nasty energy and you mirror it right back to them, later reflecting in disbelief. It's the feeling that comes when you wake up late, spill your coffee getting in the car, get a flat tire heading to work, your boss is calling incessantly, and then you end up missing the possible career changing presentation you had been working on for months.

When catabolic energy is present, your body sets off cortisol and adrenaline in hopes of making it through. This fight or flight response is available to you for temporary use, yet people often find themselves living in this space for days, weeks, months, even decades with zero conscious awareness, simply because they've normalized it. They have normalized the presence of cortisol pumping through their veins and the feeling adrenaline brings as it invades their neurology. This is the same energy that people who seek out drama are just trying to get a fix of. Just one more crime show. Just one more slow roll by the gruesome car accident. Just one more belligerent conversation on a talk show. Just one more gos-sipy conversation with friends so the adrenaline keeps flowing and the normalized vibe carries on.[25]

When I tell you that catabolic energy is addictive and ca-pable of hijacking your entire life, believe me. You would be astounded to know how common normalizing the presence of adrenaline is and how often you continually seek it out as a soothing mechanism, as there is no other feeling that produc-es the same results. Catabolic energy is incredibly paralyzing and often fills you with heavy feelings.

When you find yourself victim to catabolic energy, it would behoove you to place your full and complete attention on finding a way to shift out of that energy as soon as possible. Contracted, catabolic energy, may be placed on your map with or without intention. It is either unknowingly deposited by somebody who also felt contracted in that space, or it was deposited by someone who had a perspective of you from their map that appeared contracted.

Catabolic energy is only destructive when it starts over-taking your life. Using it as a tool to move from one space to another is necessary. If you are using it with great intention, it can be as incredibly powerful as anabolic energy. Catabolic energy is what moves people from paralyzed victims into angry action-takers. Social justice is great evidence of this. Social justice was built with intention from catabolic energy in an angry response to injustice. Using it with intention and channeling your anger towards a solution is powerful. Being a victim to it and remaining paralyzed is how people get *stuck*. Imagine how much more sense this word makes now when people tell you they feel stuck. Their physiology and neurolo-gy are layered in paralyzed energy, in an old fight or flight pat-tern, and they do not see any other choice but the one that's there—and it's not working. This brings us to level one energy.

PAUSE WITH JODEE: I understand I have provided a great deal of content in this book that may have felt abstract. Those moments were followed with intentional analogies that allowed you to integrate and understand that information at a higher level. This chapter is usually the pivotal space where everything comes together. If it does not make sense to you, know that that is normal. Because you have normalized your map, your energy, your responses, your values, your beliefs and your thoughts, they will not feel out of place or even responsible for your outcome. Know that over time this will all sink in.

Understanding and learning levels of awareness will either immediately click for you or it will leave you a bit confused. Much like everything else on this planet, it will take time to create awareness around how and where these show up in your life. There's no way around this content. The more you learn about the law of vibration and the levels of energy, the easier your life will become.

If you are unsure where your energy lies, pick up your phone. What are the last five songs you listened to? Who are you following and what are you sharing on social media? What's cued up on your TV to watch when you get home from work? How do you spend your downtime and who do you spend it with? Those answers are clear evidence of where your default energy lies. And if you are looking for a return on your energy, you first have to know where it is.

Level One

Level One (L1) energy is rooted in and fueled by shame. When you experience this LOE you feel powerless, guilty, embarrassed, anxious, in judgment of self, heavy and what most people refer to as *stuck*. L1 energy is 100 percent catabolic, leaving you feeling utterly contracted and unable to find a solution. It's the space where you feel like you are a victim without choices. It's the part of your map where you feel you are at the lowest point. It's as if you are stuck in a hole, unable to climb out. You also often feel as if you were put here against your will. It's like wearing glasses, yet the lenses are blacked out, leaving you with no vision. It's incredibly common for someone who is experiencing L1 energy to seek out some L4 energy.

The advantage of experiencing L1 energy is that it's a perfect level for self-protection. If you are outside of choice, the fault cannot be yours. If you have no responsibility around the situation, you cannot be held responsible for what results. L1 energy allows you to rest and heal because you are completely disconnected from the outcome and any accountability it may bring. L1 energy also allows you to receive sympathy from any observers who may be witnessing the process. Sympathy is often mistaken for small bursts of anabolic energy, yet it is not. Take note that sympathy and empathy are two different things. Sympathy generates from a lower LOE, often from unconscious, displaced shame—you poor thing, I feel so bad for you, you don't deserve this. These statements are deeply rooted in shame. Whereas empathy comes from a higher LOE and offers positive, forward-moving support. It literally feels lighter.[26]

Level Two

Level Two (L2) energy is rooted in anger and hostility. When you are experiencing L2 energy, you are defiant, aggressive, frustrated and full of blame. L2 energy causes you to micro-manage people. It's loaded with resentment, resistance, and hyper focused on what's broken. You will know you are experiencing L2 energy when you find it difficult to trust others and you shift into isolation. From an L2, everything you see is fire. You experience misplaced anger, see everything as a conflict, and stay in a pissed off, ready-to-fight state of mind. If you were wearing glasses, the lenses would be red, fueled by aggression and fire.

The advantage to L2 is that it can be incredibly motivating. Because there is so much anger present, you are moved to action. As shared earlier, social justice emanates from an L2 energy. It creates incredible competitive energy, and you tend to get a lot accomplished from this level.

L1 and L2 energies are both highly unconscious levels, and when you are experiencing them, you have no idea you are in them. The more you run one of these unhealthy, unproductive and dangerous patterns, the more you normalize them. Because you have normalized that feeling and the access to them is highly unconscious, these patterns are often mistaken for a biological or chemical imbalance versus a learned behavior. Due to that normalization, these are the exact spaces you may attempt to medicate. These are also the LOE that make drugs so addictive. Drugs and alcohol numb these lower LOE, allowing the addict to not feel shame, blame, anger, etc. Knowing what you know now, how does that change your perspective?

Behaviors are a symptom of the problem;
they are not the actual problem.

—DR. RICHARD BANDLER

Medicating behaviors is simply medicating the symptoms. It soothes the symptom yet never addresses the actual root cause. As shared previously, medicating behaviors is kind of like throwing someone a life preserver. The medication, in that moment, is a temporary solution to a life-altering challenge. Making that life preserver a permanent fixture is not sustainable nor does it move you forward. It simply reduces your ability to feel things and experience things, including many of the good things. Because the tree won't bear lemons, we medicate it. Or, because we can't get the desired behavior out of a person—or ourselves—let's medicate them instead of investigating what layer or root cause is preventing the outcome they so desperately desire. You can unlearn learned behaviors.

Level Three

Level Three (L3) is the first level that includes anabolic energy. Although it only comes in a small dose, it allows you to begin justifying and rationalizing what's going on around you. This is your first introduction to self-awareness, creating the idea that there may be choice involved. It's from this LOE that people tolerate, manipulate, compromise. It's from this space that people start functioning from their head instead of their heart. Because manipulation and rationalization play such a huge role here, this is where entitlement is born. L3 allows you to make excuses and exercise forgiveness. You find yourself saying things like *it is what it is*. If you were wearing glasses, the L3 lenses would be rose colored, as everything can be justified, rationalized or manipulated to fit the need at hand.

People who experience dominant L3 energy tend to decorate their exterior. They tend to buy expensive clothing, cars, and houses to hide the flaws they feel internally. Their personal appearance is always on point and they believe that if they decorate it, it will hide the way they feel inside. It does not matter how many name brands you place on your body or what kind of car you drive, people with higher levels of energy can pick up on this from a mile away. Hiding your external does not upgrade your internal, it simply attracts more people that hide, further exacerbating your challenge. Remember, energy self-levels. With that in mind, how does your current LOE impact the people you attract?

The advantages of L3 are that you are always looking for the silver lining, the lesson learned and the space to say it's good enough. People with high amounts of level three do not allow other people to hold them back. They have enough self-awareness to understand that even if someone has told them something is or is not possible, they persevere.

Level Four

Level Four (L4) is what I often refer to as the conscious middle. There is a ton of content here, as this is where most of the population settles. L4 is the land of the *fixers*. It's where compassion overflows. It's the level where acceptance is found and sympathy is born. It's the space where you will find supportive yet over-involved, over-functioning energy. When people are experiencing L4 energy, they just want to make it better. They feel selfless and thrive in their old stories. The stories are laden with catabolic energy that they overcame.

This level is unconsciously full of judgment, as people often want to help others because they know how they feel. People with high L4 energy burnout the fastest because of this constant need to help others.

This level of energy is where most people unknowingly get stuck because they mistake it for L7. Because L4 is a fifty-fifty mix, half catabolic and half anabolic, it's the most anabolic energy they've experienced thus far. Due to this, people experiencing L4 often believe that they can *fix* others or believe they have solved the challenge that landed them here. Because of this, people who have a predominant amount of L4 energy often over-function for people who are under-functioning. There is an incredibly unhealthy loop that happens between people with predominant L4 energy and people with predominant L1 energy. The L1 energy is always looking for someone to fix them, and L4 energy is always looking for someone to fix. This creates an unhealthy loop where both participants are consistently getting what I refer to as the chemical payoff. It's this same cycle that fuels codependency. Codependency is not anabolic; it's actually incredibly catabolic.

When predominant L4 energy is present, you may get overly emotional when someone else experiences a heavy emotion. You may shift into this sympathetic, hovering, oh you must feel so sad or so bad or so empty energy. Then you unload insane amounts of catabolic energy into the person who is trying to process and heal. This delays their ability to process and heal and further emotionally incapacitates them. Yet it's a weird relief for the L4 fixer. This is terribly dangerous and is the pivotal space that leads to arrested emotional development (AED). (more on AED in chapter 13)

Dominant level four energy creates a constant need and desire to change people so they fit in inside your map of the world, completely negating their map or their opportunity to experience the territory independently. L4 energy protects the ego, which believes if I don't stay here and help you along, you will fail. This need to help is a trauma response and grows from a place of unprocessed trauma. There is something present on your map that never received proper acknowledgment and validation, leaving you with an unhealed wound that constantly needs to be soothed. This is harmful, and it's what I refer to as scissor syndrome.

Scissor Syndrome™

Scissor Syndrome is often associated with L4 energy. Imagine that you are enjoying the outdoors and you find the most beautiful caterpillar all nestled up in his cocoon. You have noticed the cocoon a few times, and as you watch him day after day, you begin to believe he's struggling. He has this gigantic cocoon surrounding him and he can't seem to get it off. You know from a scientific perspective that all he wants to do is fly. You feel so bad watching his attempts to escape. He is just struggling and struggling day after day after day. You've watched and witnessed his attempts, yet he is never successful. You know that if you could just help him, he could be free and fly away.

You take it upon yourself to free him. You pull out your scissors and start snipping away his cocoon, granting his wish for freedom that he is so desperately seeking. Yet as he attempts to fly away, he falls to the ground. He keeps trying to fly, yet his wings are just not strong enough. He ends up returning to the cocoon for shelter as he is unable to fly. The thing you never realized was that he was doing exactly what he was supposed to do to learn how to fly, yet it was too much for you to witness. His struggle triggered something in you.

Unbeknownst to you, each time he pushed on that cocoon it was building muscle for him. And each time he wasn't successful it built resiliency. He got a bit more mentally strong with each failed attempt. It is the pushing and pushing and pushing on the cocoon and learning through the struggle that builds the physical strength, courage and character necessary for flying. All of which is incredibly necessary to not only survive but also thrive in the big world. Yet your inability to witness that struggle forever stunted his ability to grow.

It's not that he was under-functioning; he was doing his job. He was doing exactly what every other butterfly did to earn their wings. It was just too much for you to witness, so you chose to over-function, soothe your old wound and your old, unprocessed feelings, and *fix* it. Saving other people from themselves is not helpful! It simply keeps them in peril. When you save people to soothe your needs, you rob them of the learning opportunities they need to grow. Imagine if every time you sat down to do a crossword puzzle all the answers were already there, just faintly etched in the boxes. Would you still want to play? Probably not, because the reason you play is for the quick, short chemical bursts that feed your anabolic energy. When those endorphins saturate your brain, you feel happy. You feel accomplished. There is no substitute for that. You intentionally and unconsciously seek out those anabolic moments, as they are necessary for healthy growth.

Over-functioning robs the other person from ever experiencing that chemical payoff, that natural high, so they eventually stop trying. When you interrupt that process for another person by giving them the answer, helping them not struggle or stepping into their map and decorating it from your map, you are harming them and holding them back. You are trying to fix them because *your* map feels out of control in that space, not theirs. Your strategy will not work on someone else because it's *your* strategy. Your crayons of experience are not capable of coloring other people's maps. You are worthy of releasing your own trauma. Put the scissors down and heal your own map.

Know Your Shadow

There's something about L4 energy that people get stuck in. It's one of those fascinating spaces and often reminds me of Carl Jung's shadow theory. L4 energy and the Conscious Middle remind you of who you used to be. They connect the idea that there is often an unconscious presence of who you used to be, and your ego is struggling to release it. The presence of that old energy draws people back into your life who are currently experiencing the things you have mastered and grown from, and you inevitably believe they need your help. The combination of your old story and their present need creates an opportunity L4s simply cannot resist.

Default L4 fixers feel compelled to pause their own personal growth and progress and begin helping the people who are experiencing the lower LOEs, starting with L1. The reason this happens is because high levels of L4 energy bring self-identified expertise in L1, L2, and L3; and in their mind, it makes sense to *help* others. The L4 shadow is so predominant in this LOE because there is still some unknown, unprocessed trauma lingering or a shadow that is triggered by witnessing others in similar situations, leading you to believe your assistance is needed. Know that it is not needed. Once that piece of trauma is identified, processed, and healed, your shadow will dissipate, your lenses will change, and you will transcend to L5, forever seeing the world differently. Until that occurs, you will continually attempt to rescue and fix people, unknowingly harming them further.

The advantage of L4 energy is that it allows you to extend yourself and help others. The key to that space is establishing and honoring your boundaries as well as honoring other people's healing journeys and allowing them to heal in their own way.

Level Five

People who lead with Level Five (L5) energy are visionaries and are seeking collaboration. L5 brings a moderate amount of anabolic energy. The presence of this energy allows you to be calm in the face of adversity, capable of dividing and conquering. You become solution-oriented and are moved to action. You are constantly finding ways to create peace and fluidity in yourself and others. You bring incredible, poised power both professionally and personally, and you view opportunities everywhere. Your judgment dissipates and you become a conscious observer of your own life. Your boundaries are strong. Your self-care is built in, and you see everyone around you as gifted. You lead with curiosity and fearlessness.

L5 energy creates a space where you lead more with your head and less with your heart. It's more logical, less emotional. Viewing everything with pure and utter curiosity allows you to be free from judgment and committed to the solution. Your focus is to simply move forward and forge on. Regardless of the challenges you find, you see everything as fixable. This is where the idea you either win, or you learn emanates from. There's always something to learn from your past endeavors. Keep the lesson, release the emotion and carry on.

It's at this LOE that you begin experiencing Intentional Consciousness. You begin deliberately commanding and controlling your default energy, your state of mind, because you wholeheartedly understand the impact it has on your world. You have healed your past wounds and made peace with how they changed you. From that space, you understand the world around you just a bit more. From the L4 section, you are incredibly fluent in your physiology and understand how things affect you. At L5, you are now at choice as to how you want to respond to the world around you. You believe the world is your oyster. You have zero desire to fix anyone because no one is broken. Everyone is exactly where they are supposed to be. You trust that everyone can take care of themselves and that if they need help, they will ask for it. You are present in the moment, yet do not have to be in charge. You often lead from the back. You are in charge of your own energy, as everyone is in charge of theirs. Nothing is broken; there is nothing to fix.

When you have predominant L5 energy, you intentionally spend time resonating inside what you want, what you are looking for and how you will acquire it. You set goals and you stay on the path. You are a conscious leader who gets stuff done. You are conscious of what it takes to lead, what it takes to stay engaged and what it takes to succeed. You stay incredibly conscious of the places and the things that feed your energy and intentionally avoid the things that deplete it.

The advantage to L5 energy is that it brings a permanent sense of peace. It allows you to have strong boundaries, and modeling it encourages others to build theirs as well. You are a full-on team player and you are detached from the outcome. Your curiosity allows you to lead others from a place disconnected from judgment and open to new ideas, furthering your growth and theirs.

Level Six

At Level Six (L6), everyone wins. This level reminds me of the Oprah moment, "You get a car, and you get a car, and you get a car." It's endless and relentless feelings of optimism and synergy. If you win, we are all winning. People who have high L6 energy intentionally choose this level. You rise above with great intention. You are completely conscious of exactly what you want in your world, what you want your world to look like, and you choose the LOE that coordinates with it. L6 is a highly intentional, high-functioning, high-performing level.

L6 and L7 energy are completely conscious energies. L6 energy is powered and led by intuition. When you are experiencing L6 energy, you simply know things and can feel your way through versus needing instruction or external guidance. L6 energy is where optimism is born. It's not that you are being optimistic, it's that optimism is simply your default outlook on life. You know that anything is possible and that everyone has the power. From that space, you detach. You have a global perspective and being in the flow is your default state. You find purpose in everything. You are innovative and connected. You are a community builder, and people come to you for the prolific wisdom you share.

Judgment is not present in your energy, as you are an empathetic, anabolic leader. You are engaged and powerful from a soulful, purpose-driven space instead of an egocentric space. You find heavy, lingering, catabolic energy stagnant and you avoid it. You may often appear aloof or disconnected because of your intentional detachment from catabolic energy and the drama it brings. You have strong, intentional boundaries around your energy and you protect them. You are healed and whole, allowing everyone to walk their own path in their own time, free from your involvement. You are resilient, engaged and incredibly creative.

L6 energy brings permanent feelings of joy to you. You find yourself in the equation and in the answer as you are a connected, engaged leader. What also comes with that territory is that you are a very high risk-taker. Because you believe everything is fixable and that everything will work itself out, you take huge risks that others may perceive as ludicrous. You also have the ability to lead with empathy that's free from judgment or *fixing* energy. Leading from this L6 energy builds incredible communities. A disadvantage to L6 energy is that others often try to contract you because they are envious of your expansion. Stay conscious of your healing journey.

An advantage to L6 energy is the ability to find synergy in all things. You believe everything happens because it's supposed to, and everyone is exactly where they should be, so you make decisions from that default space. Because of your permanent sense of joy, you have the ability to create happiness from the inside out and do not need external decorations, stimulus or energy from others. This creates fierce independence.

Level Seven

Picture the energy that happens when your team makes that odds-defying game point and the entire stadium erupts into madness. It doesn't matter if you know the guy next to you or not—in that moment, all of a sudden, everyone is your best friend. You're hugging strangers. High fiving everyone. Literally high on life. You are invincible and disconnected from reality. That is 100 percent pure anabolic energy. The incredible amounts of anabolic energy offered at L7 are also found in meditative states, in creative states, and in anything that allows you to disconnect from your routines and your patterns.

L7 energy is bliss. It's where you find your Zen. It's the place you go to when you lose all track of time and space. According to Esther Hicks, it is when you are *in the flow*. Nothing phases you. There are no barriers, no rules—just wide-open space to create. It makes sense if this all sounds too good to be true. Although L7 energy is available, it is not sustainable full-time. Unless of course you are in a constant meditative state. You unknowingly find yourself in L7 energy when you are disconnected from your normal routine—in times when you are out to dinner with an old friend, putting together a puzzle, painting, walking, swimming, doing yoga, golfing, fishing or doing whatever it is that allows that creative freedom. That is the closest you get to your truest self.[27]

When you are in your L7 energy, you can experience emotions without judgment. You are fearless and in a space where you can consciously create your life. You create brilliant things out of nothing and spontaneously manifest things, as you are experiencing absolute passion. People who have high levels of L7 energy are the most powerful people in the world.[28]

Energetic Patterns

Now that you are aware of how energy works, recognize how each respective level shows up in your life. If you feel like you are constantly attracting drama, where is the root source in your pattern? If you have energy that someone doesn't like you, pleasing other people doesn't negate that original feeling.

If you have feelings that you are not pretty enough, tall enough, short enough, smart enough or simply just enough, decorating your exterior and masking the pain only masks the pain. It doesn't speak to it or change the root cause. Remember that energy self-levels, and you're inevitably going to attract people who feel the same way and are masking the same pain, further delaying your personal growth. This cyclical pattern continues to run as you burn your energy out trying to fix them or let them fix you by soothing the old stories. If this is resonating and making sense to you, it means it's in your energetic pattern. If this does not make sense to you, appreciate the moment.

If you have frustration or anger from your childhood pattern and the layers it has created, figure out the story you've built around it and how it shows up in your everyday life. I recently heard Dr. Wayne Dyer share, "Do you want to live ninety years, or do you want to live the same year ninety times?"[29] That hit me to my core. It's a great reminder of how we normalize keeping old memories present and unconsciously allowing them to make our decisions.[33]

You and you alone are the only thing that can impact your energy. HARD STOP.

No one outside of you can change the way you feel. If you believe that others can change the way you feel, know that it's a temporary space. If your energy rises when certain people are around, it's because of what you're allowing yourself to believe when they are present. The idea here is learning to believe, even with them not present, the things they bring out in you are still true. Those qualities are completely independent from the people who highlight them for you. Learning and being intentional about how and where you find evidence of that goodness is a journey only for you. The more you can access those parts of you, the more you will want to find them.

The reason your first love always holds so much space in your energy is because that's the first time you learned that much about yourself. It was the first time you learned what that kind of love felt like. You often equate that amount of love to the other person or give your power away to that person, believing that without them present you are not happy. Know that the love you felt was yours. It was your pure energy brought to the surface by the presence of someone else, yet it was yours from the start. Find the path that allows you that same access.

Energy Awareness Takeaways

➤ When you are in survival mode, you have no idea you are there. Creating awareness around what triggers you and/or the patterns that you create is how sustainable change happens.

➤ The way to consciously shift your energy is through awareness and intention.

➤ What are the lenses that you view the world through made of? If your default setting is rooted in shame, you will view everything through a shame lens.

➤ When you are decorating your external world it's because you're internally unconscious.

➤ When you are completely conscious internally, your external world disappears.

➤ Healing is a mind and body connection.

➤ People cannot make you feel bad. You choose to respond to the energy they are offering.

➤ How is your reality creating who you attract?

> ➢ Create awareness around what LOE you are modeling and expecting from your kids, parents, spouse, coworkers and/or employees.

> ➢ Stay conscious of what LOE you process content in.

> ➢ Start paying attention to the things that contract you and the things that allow you to expand.

> ➢ When you set an intentional LOE, take note of who stays and who vacates.

> ➢ Get fluent in the things that engage your fight or flight response. How do you know when the cortisol and adrenaline start to flow?

> ➢ Get fluent in the things that soothe your old story. Know when and what causes your endorphins to start flowing.

> ➢ Become aware of where your energy is aligned and how it keeps you safe from being, doing or feeling something.

> ➢ The more you suppress unprocessed energy, the more it continues to come out in more and more unhealthy ways.

> ➢ Learn to understand that things are not right or wrong, they're simply different.

> ➢ And the biggest takeaway: people can only experience you from their highest LOE.

When you start to understand your own vibrational patterns, it creates an awareness like no other. Take note of what triggers these and what they feel like inside your body. This is how you create Intentional Consciousness. Your vibration of truth is when the universe continues to show you the good, yet you keep pushing it back.

Understand your vibration of shame/victim mode

Understand your vibration of anger

Understand your vibration of justification

Understand your vibration of fixing others

Understand your vibration of synergy

Understand your vibration of detached involvement

Understand your vibration of absolute enlightenment

When you start understanding where your energy is, are you standing on the wrap around porch with a 360-degree view of the world, or are you standing behind a door, attempting to take the entire world in through a peephole?

Oftentimes people make big assumptions about other people, expecting a certain behavior, a certain response or a certain outcome. The biggest challenge with this assumption is embracing the idea that people would first have to have access to that LOE in order to respond in that certain way. Remember, what keeps people outside of their goals or their ideal performance is rarely skill level. It's almost always the LOE in which they are processing what's possible. A catabolic equation does not provide an anabolic response.

The Topography of Your Map

The topography of your map lies in the law of vibration. Remember that the map you started with was blank and a great deal of content was added without your knowledge and or awareness. Knowing what you know now, identify where the lower LOE are. Imagine they're like potholes, wreaking havoc on your system each time you experience them.

Remember that energy self-levels. If you don't like the situation you are in, check the LOE first. Investigate its roots and understand how the energetic pattern works. If you are not liking certain people that you keep drawing in, check and see what LOE you have in common with them or what old pattern you're still running that creates that common thread. Know what your LOE is offering. Know what LOE you are emitting in each different circle and facet of your life. It's quite possible you are an L6 CEO at work and an L1 parent. It's absolutely possible you've normalized that juxtaposed energy and it's burning you out. Get fluent in the spaces in your life where your audio does not match your video and find the roots.

Also know that life's a journey and we are all doing the very best we can with the map we are currently using. Believe that people's intentions are always pure. And even though there are times that it feels quite the opposite, everyone is searching for peace, love and connection, even in the darkest of places.

Questions for Insight

➤ How conscious are you of your LOE?

_____

_____

➤ Where does your default LOE rest?

_____

_____

➢ How does that default LOE serve you?

➢ At what LOE do you find the most access
to yourself?

➢ How does your childhood story impact your LOE?

➢ What could you allow yourself to believe now that
allows that energy to dissipate?

Chapter 10

Anchors & Triggers— Stop Pushing My Buttons!

Remember the scenario that opened chapter 8? The one where you're moving about your day, minding your own business, when out of nowhere that voice hits you and you immediately feel hijacked? It's uncomfortable and your body responds before you are even aware of it, and you know something is vehemently pushing your buttons.

A trigger, what we sometimes call a button, is an unconscious response that engages your nervous system when a similar stimulus appears. The trigger engages what is known as an anchor, or the root cause. In chapter 8, we discussed how we take the world in through our five senses (KAVOG). Triggers are what happens when you unknowingly experience one or more of those five senses in an identical or close to identical pattern and in the way it was originally anchored— think sight of a dog, phone ringing incessantly, coworker demanding a response, etc.

This replication of the original event causes your nervous system to immediately respond, often in the identical way it was encoded on your map the first time. It follows the same TEA pattern. It starts with a thought that pulls forward an emotion and ends with your response, your behavior. Meaning, if you were frustrated the first time, you will be frustrated this time. If you were angry the first time, anger will appear again. It's an energetic pattern that simply repeats itself on cue. Whether it's the way bananas smell, the sound of gunfire, the sight of a dog, the feeling you get when you enter a small, confined space, the smell of a hospital room or the sight of blood, in each event your physiology and neurology both respond before you do.

Your nervous system is laden with anchors awaiting a trigger. Each one of these highly personalized and subjective anchored events have a root cause that only you know. If you were ever an athlete, the sound of a whistle blowing might mean something completely different to you than it would to someone who never played sports. If you are a parent, a child's cry sounds so different when it's your child that's crying versus a stranger's. If you are a diehard sports fan, the sound of a game in full swing sets your soul on fire. And if you've ever been or are still in an incredible relationship, the first note of that one song, the smell of your partner's clothing or the energy of their presence evokes your neurology like nothing else can. Although this is a miniscule glimpse, these are all examples of anchors that lie dormant until they are engaged. You have thousands of anchors. When the anchor is awakened from its slumber, whether that be a half a day or three decades later, the response is always the same.

What Is an Anchor?

As briefly mentioned in chapter 3, over the course of your life, multiple anchors have unknowingly been installed onto your map that are triggered in your daily life. Anchors are the remnants left behind from your previous experiences. They are directly related to a root cause or layer that occurred previously in your life. Anchors can be simple and installed within minutes or built over time, taking years to master and can lie dormant for decades at a time. Think about how quickly your physiology responds when learning the rules, cadence, posture or flow of a new game, a new song or a new dance. And how quickly those same memorized patterns can come rushing back in decades later without warning. I'm embarrassed to share that the first thing that came to mind as I typed that sentence was the macarena. As soon as the song starts playing, everyone knows the dance.

Much like the macarena, the consistent repeating of a pattern builds a presence in your physiology that, when minimally provoked, creates a rippled, unconscious result—riding a bike, changing a diaper, sweeping the floor, raking leaves, etc. These are what we refer to in the world of NLP as anchors. An anchor is in essence any representation, internally or externally generated, which triggers another representation. When you experience the internal or external trigger, engaging the original anchor, you are moved into action, unconsciously and without notice.[31]

Examples of Anchors & Triggers

KAVOG Trigger then anchor	Internal/ External Trigger	Anchor (encoded memory)	Internal/External anchored Response
Auditory trigger Kinesthetic anchor	That one song	Wedding day, first kiss, funeral	The mirrored emotion of the moment it was encoded
Kinesthetic trigger Kinesthetic anchor	Feels like riding a bike	Remembering how to ride	Balance, pedal-ing, posture
Auditory trigger Kinesthetic anchor	Angry voices	Verbal abuse	Terrified, contracted and closed energy, fight or flight engaged
Auditory trigger Kinesthetic anchor	Screaming baby	Maybe a fresh dia-per will work	Change the baby's diaper
Auditory trigger Kinesthetic anchor	Sound of a whistle	Line up, start, stop	Creates awareness to pay attention
Visual trigger Kinesthetic anchor	Sight of blood	Childhood injury or sight of injury	Nauseous, faint
Kinesthetic trigger Kinesthetic anchor	Someone hands you a broom	Brooms are for sweeping	You start sweeping
Olfactory trigger Kinesthetic anchor	Smell of banana	Mandated eat-ing as a child	Anger, frustrat-ed, refusal

The list is endless. The little things and the big things have all unknowingly been anchored on your map and can be called forward in a moment's notice. The only thing necessary to call them forward is the identical representational system that they were originally encoded in. If someone hands you a broom, you're probably going to start sweeping, not try to brush your teeth with it. If someone hands you a crying baby, the first thing you might check is their diaper. If someone hands you a bike and says, let's go, you're probably not going to put the bike on your back and start walking. Your brain knows that bikes are for riding, brooms are for sweeping and babies cry when they are uncomfortable. So even if you haven't ridden a bike in ten years, the memory of how to do so is anchored on your map, as is your ability to use a broom and change a diaper. The original event and the idea that you know what to do with these items immediately comes back, so do all the other things that have been unknowingly anchored onto your map.

Although it may sound redundant, the more heightened an emotion, the deeper the anchor is embedded. It's not always about the consistency of the pattern or the number of times you've used it; it's always about the intensity in which it was encoded. Much like your first love, that moment is anchored into your neurology because it's the first time you intensely experienced that deep of an emotion. That anchor is now deeply embedded on your map with the person it involved. Each and every time you hear that person's name, remember those moments or revisit the places you enjoyed with them, those heightened emotions come rushing back in.

You may open and close your front door a thousand times in a year, and it doesn't even phase you. Yet someone else's front door? Now that might strike a chord. Because it's that front door that you were standing at when you received the news, or that's the front door you were at when you broke your arm, or that's the front door that you were standing at when you were unexpectedly attacked. That door is now for-ever associated and anchored with the event that caused the heightened emotion. Remember, the more heightened the emotion, the deeper the anchor.

Your map reveals the emotions that you keep anchored down, deep inside your story. The lessons you learn and the things that are added to your map are not who you are; they're simply where you've been. If you survived child ne-glect or spousal abuse or fleeing from your native country or even war, you are not those things. Those things are simply holding space on your map, with an incredibly deep anchor. As soon as you gain conscious awareness of them, you can then take intentional steps towards healing those spaces and then decide, when you're ready, to release the energy around them. These memories only remain big and strong because of the LOE you place on them. HARD STOP.

Button pushing, triggers and the way you respond to the people around you are 100 percent in alignment with what's currently anchored on your map. When you are triggered, it's because something on your map is unhealed; it's not about the other person. Once the buttons are disarmed or the ener-gy behind the trigger is removed, they no longer define who you are. When you recall those moments, they no longer hi-jack your neurology. They simply become parts of your jour-ney, flattened areas on your map, that hold memories instead of heavy, frenetic energy. The front door won't matter. The sound of a whistle will blend in with all the other background noises, and that one memory will no longer phase you.

The goal of this chapter is to provide you with an under-standing of how buttons and triggers are created, why this cause-and-effect reaction exists, how to create intentional awareness around them and how to release them from your map. Although the only awareness you may have around these triggered events is the reaction they bring, know that you can be intentionally conscious in how you respond, co-creating your reality versus unconsciously responding.

Stop Pushing My Buttons

Buttons are basically anchored beliefs. They've been anchored into our nervous system from either repetition or because at the moment of installation there was high, intense emotion present. Buttons are simply another word for triggers. Oftentimes you'll hear people say he's pushing my buttons or she's pushing my buttons. The first questions I ask as a coach are:

➤ What would happen if the button wasn't there?

➤ Who installed the button?

➤ Who can remove the button?

Imagine what it would feel like to not respond to that button. The only reason why another human can push your buttons is because your buttons are available and alive. The source of that response lives inside you. Once you create awareness that the button does not control you, yet instead you control the button, your life will change. This internal versus external view is powerful. Once your buttons or your anchors are released, removed, or desensitized, they will no longer be available to engage with. They simply won't work. The opposite is also true. Until your buttons are released, removed or desensitized they will continue to run your life. Also, once a button has been engaged or an anchor has been triggered and you have been activated, it's challenging to make a conscious decision from that emotionally heightened state. It's like attempting to put out a forest fire with a garden hose. It may sound like a good idea, but it's not very effective.

Emotions only last for roughly ninety seconds. Staying in them any longer is simply a choice. Even giving yourself a full five minutes to resonate and process what just happened may sometimes be necessary. For example, if you are in traffic and someone cuts you off, you either choose to slow down a bit and let them in, keeping yourself safe, or you hold steady on the gas, challenging their power, allowing them to frustrate you and engage in their ridiculous behavior. Both are a choice. The energy around the emotions that emanate from either dissipates after about ninety seconds. The emotion is only charged when you create a story around them. That story then creates a thought and the TEA starts spilling. The choice is always yours.

The most powerful thing that can change your outcome is the awareness that you create around what triggers you. Get in front of these spaces. There is no person on the planet that understands your triggers like you do. There's no other person on the planet who has an encoded, layered map that matches yours. There is no other person on the planet that has the same visceral responses to external and internal stimuli that you do. Your map is yours. Your layered map was created from your life experience. Understanding and creating aware-ness around what triggers you is one of the most powerful steps you can take in consciously shifting your level of energy (LOE). This is how sustainable change is created.

The reason buttons and triggers are so powerful is because they take you back to that exact moment when that button or trigger was encoded. If that encoded anchor created a fight or flight response for you, each and every time you experience a trigger or a button similar to the original one, it engages an identical energetic pattern. The same emotional response will erupt, and you will be thrown right back into fight or flight without warning or intention. Your daily actions also reinforce your anchors each and every time you repeat the patterns, consciously and unconsciously.

You align yourself, your life, your extracurricular activities and your vibe with people who have similar maps, similar beliefs and energies and have also normalized the presence of triggering events. Know that redesigning and editing your map is just as easy as reinforcing it. It just takes intentional effort. If you are normalizing verbal abuse and you hang around with people that either allow the abuse or are the abuser, the verbal commentary may not stand out as triggering until someone outside of the group speaks in that manner. Or vice versa, if you're used to people speaking kindly it's absolutely going to stand out when someone does not use kind words. What you have anchored on your map is kindness, so when someone is out of alignment with that kindness, it stands out to you—it's triggering.

You have a multitude of things anchored on your map, some positive and some negative. Remember that these are not right or wrong, they're simply different from each other. Anchoring kindness on your map absolutely serves you. When you find evidence of kindness in the world, it illuminates that area of your map, your brain is saturated with endorphins, and you remember how kind the world really is. Anchoring negativity on your map is similar to housing an open wound. It's the psychological sunburn. Imagine how a miniscule movement can evoke the biggest response when a sunburn is still smoldering. Yet if you have normalized the pain, overtime it doesn't even phase you. You're used to getting burned. You're used to feeling pain. You may have even conceded that it's tied to your worthiness and begin expecting it, awaiting the pain. Pain is not normal, and continually getting burned is not a way of life. These anchors will be released once they are acknowledged, validated, and processed.

Know in those moments, those words are not about you, they are more in alignment with what is anchored on the other person's map. This is what I meant by the power of words. If that part of your map is raw, oozing, intensely heightened, full of color, sound turned all the way up and as frenetic as possible, when someone speaks words into it that trigger you, and you blame the person for speaking the words, it's your map my friend. The reason you are triggered by the things that other people say is because it's already alive and well on your map. You are unconsciously feeding it with your thoughts, keeping it alive; and as soon as somebody provokes it, your world crumbles. Sustainable change comes from healing the map and taking your power back. Scolding the speaker only further exacerbates the challenge.

In direct alignment with everything I have shared thus far, understand that you can only be triggered by something that is presently on your map. Although that may feel out of access or out of alignment with your current thought process, remember that your map is as old as you are. You've had anchors placed along your map throughout your entire life, without your conscious awareness or knowledge. The presence of those anchors has created a level of normalcy that you are not aware of. As shared earlier, if you are an only child and hail from a quiet household, that quiet space is normal space for you. You may struggle in places that you believe are too loud, too frenetic, too unsettled, while unbeknownst to you, the person you are with feels right at home with all of it. Maybe your friend has a handful of siblings and grew up in an incredibly chaotic household. The background noise of the restaurant and the energy of all the people there does not even phase them. It's simply an average day out. Old, anchored memories may be the exact thing that is challenging you, yet because it's something you have utterly normalized it does not stand out to you.

Why Anchors Matter

Anchors matter because they represent that space you once believed was out of access. They represent automatic responses and the idea of that's just who I am versus now understanding this anchor is still alive on my map because I have not had the access to it and/or the skills to process it. Once you can access and process each anchor, your awareness shifts from external to internal. Once you process your anchors you realize the external world is not commanding your reality, instead it's your internal representation of what you are absorbing externally. It circles back to one of my favorite questions: What are you making that mean? Often when my clients are triggered, I will ask that question right in that moment. What are you making that mean? It stops them dead in their tracks and brings immediate awareness around the patterns they run and what is anchored to them.

When you realize what you and you alone make things mean, it gives you more understanding and access to your patterns. If a certain tone of voice makes you angry, unpack that anchor. It's not the tone of voice that makes you angry, it's what you're making that tone mean. You may be interpreting it as the other person disrespected you, or that person doesn't like you, or you don't deserve that tone, completely negating the history of your meaning and the other person's map. The other person may not know how to speak kindly, they may have simply been having a bad day, they may have reflected on it as soon as you walked away and had every intention of apologizing yet didn't. The idea here is that the meaning that you give to an encounter becomes the meaning of the encounter. One of my cardinal rules is everyone is always doing the best they can. My life becomes so much easier when I just assume that everyone's doing their best, even when it hurts me.

PAUSE WITH JODEE: You are doing yourself a disservice when you continually expect something from people who cannot deliver and then get frustrated that they cannot give you what you need. The reason you hang out with the people you do is because you have similar layers, similar maps and similar LOE, not because you have similar goals. If you don't like who you're attracting, check your default LOE.

Finding Anchors

It may feel challenging to look back and find anchors rather than acknowledging in the very moment that you're triggered, pausing, and asking yourself some powerful questions, like:

- ➢ How am I letting this affect me right now?
- ➢ What am I making this mean?
- ➢ How long have I made X mean Y?
- ➢ How is the story serving me?
- ➢ How is this impacting my LOE?
- ➢ And most powerfully, what level of energy is this anchor encoded in?

Once you can gain awareness around what LOE that anchor was originally encoded in, you will gain more access to yourself than ever before. It makes total sense that when the anchor is triggered and the button is engaged, you respond in the original encoded LOE. Use the abbreviated LOE chart below to gain awareness of how and where your energy goes when these anchors are awakened.

L1 energy: You feel powerless. L1 energy represents catabolic, shame, powerlessness, guilt, embarrassment, anxiety, judgment of self, heavy, stuck, victim and being without choice.

L2 energy: You feel angry. L2 energy represents anger, hostility, defiance, aggression, frustration and blame.

L3 energy: You feel the need to justify things. L3 energy represents rationalization, justification, toleration, manipulation and compromise.

L4 energy: You feel the need to fix everything. L4 energy represents compassion, acceptance, sympathy, judgment, over-functioning, codependency and fixer energy.

L5 energy: You have a solution. L5 energy represents solution-oriented thinkers, visionaries, problem-solvers, observant leaders, logic and intention.

L6 energy: You lead with anabolic intention. L6 energy represents synergy, detached involvement, empathy, optimism, high functioning, internally guided, unflappable and innovation.

L7 energy: There is no problem. L7 energy represents bliss, Zen, detached, unaffected and being free from judgment and fear.[32]

Understanding what LOE your anchors were originally encoded in awakens new awareness around how they will, or will not, continue to affect you. Once you begin understanding the roots of your behavior, it leads you to specific layers, because now you have consciousness around an understanding of how that old, ineffective, emotionally charged memory is serving you. If it's a positively anchored memory, it makes sense why that memory brings so much joy for you, or if it's a negatively anchored memory, why you may be triggered.

Pause for a moment and take some notes.

➢ What's coming up for you?

_____

_____

_____

_____

_____

➢ What anchors have you identified (both positive and negative)?

_____

_____

_____

_____

_____

_____

_____

➤ What LOE were they originally encoded in?

_____

_____

_____

_____

_____

Once you have the LOE aligned with that anchored memory, go back and explore the list below.

➤ Recognize where you feel it in your body.

➤ What KAVOG response triggers it?

➤ What KAVOG response does it pull forward?

➤ Unpack the TEA around it.

➤ Identify what value it challenges and/or serves.

➤ What beliefs have you built from that anchor?

➤ Knowing what you know now, what is it about the trigger that challenges you, and how can you allow that energy to dissipate?

Acknowledge and validate whatever response surfaces for you. Know that your map is editable, and this is how sustainable change is made. When your nervous system is acknowledged and validated, it releases the emotional bond. Trauma is like stagnant, L1, nonmoving energy. Energy that's being held—held against its will until it is righted, until it's seen, until it's acknowledged and validated. It's only then that you can release this *stuck* energy. You are allowed to edit your map and redefine your life.

---

*Resilience is the ability to bounce
back from pressure.*
—GABOR MATÉ

Moving Forward

If your map is distorted with raw, open wounds in one area, you will filter everything through that wound until it is healed. HARD STOP. Open wounds create powerful patterns and are minimally triggered. The bigger the wound, the bigger the emotional reaction. When you think of how love is anchored on your map, is it anchored in rage or is it anchored in passion? If you have an L1 anchor around love and relationships, you will attract and pull forward other L1 partners who will mirror and amplify your (in)ability to access love from an L1 energy. If you have a L2 energy around your ex, know that your kids (if present) feel that anger and will also equate L2 energy with love, parenting, child-mom or child-dad relationships and will later attract angry, aggressive partners who match what's been anchored on their map.

The more heightened an emotion, the deeper the anchored experience. If you love someone so much that it hurts, that's why it hurts so bad. Or if you were terrified as a small child, it's embedded in your DNA and it's anchored into your unconsciousness. Every time you get anywhere near an experience like that one it brings those emotions flooding back. This is what I mean by unpacking human behavior, unpacking all the buttons, triggers and anchors that go with it. Sometimes you just have to let go of that piece of your map, that part of your story, and that anchored piece of energy that is keeping that emotion present or repressed.

Pulling Anchors

Take a moment and find your emotional patterns around the day-to-day things that create your reality. What feeling comes first when you think of

- your best friend,
- your child,
- your spouse,
- your parent(s),
- your job,
- your goals,
- your finances,
- your physical fitness,
- your emotional health
- and your mental fortitude?

If each of these things were plotted on your map, what would the topography look like? Jot down next to each one what LOE it pulls forward, what LOE it offers you and what attracts you to it or repels you from it. Now having conscious awareness that everything around you is energy, the answers above may provide clues as to your emotional, energetic patterns. Creating awareness around releasing old, catabolic energy and allowing some anabolic energy to flow is necessary for interrupting old patterns and building healthy environments. Is it possible that you're trying to build an anabolic relationship with a catabolic anchor? If the anchored belief that you're stuck in has a traumatic imprinted root, odds are high you will repeat the cycle until the anchor is acknowledged and released. Know that if you cannot find a healthy environment, you can create one.

The Freedom to Heal

Imagine that you spent the majority of your life listening to stories about people sailing the beautiful, blue sea. It's finally your turn. You set sail in the ocean on the most amazing boat ever. You've been waiting your entire life to sail this ocean because everyone talks about all the stunning things they find when they are at sea. As your boat takes off you are filled with this childlike wonder, curiously excited to finally witness all the wonders of the world. After a while you start to question if you're in the right water. Everything everyone has ever talked about isn't there. How could they have shared all these beautiful things, yet you're not finding any of them? You check your notes and realize you're in the same water they were in, yet why can you not see what they described? They talked about all this fascinating sea life, sunsets, seascapes, lobster traps, whale watching, intermittent islands, more coconuts than you can count, coral reefs seen by the naked eye and some you can scuba dive down to see, yet none of it is visible to you. What's going on? Why can you not see what they described? Disappointed, you head home. You connect with your friend and they confirm that it's all there. They repeat the story and describe it all over again. You oblige and try again. Maybe you just missed it the first time around.

The second time you set out you're determined to see everything. You think to yourself it all has to be here somewhere. You try a different route. Still nothing. You have gone back to port and tried every channel. Nothing. Embarrassed to share this with your friends, your plan is to try again in the morning. Days pass and you try each and every day to no avail. It feels like you're just moving in circles. You have given it everything you have, yet you still cannot access what they've described.

As you are headed back in from another frustrating day, ready to give up, a nearby boater passes by and shouts, "Hey buddy! Did you know your anchor's down?"

"My anchor is what!" It's at that moment you realize your anchor *is* down. It has been down this entire time, causing you to spin in a circle only moving as far as the anchor allows. You have spent all this time believing you were *out to sea* only to learn you really never even left shore. How many times in life have you attempted to do something new while simultaneously and unconsciously being committed to an old, anchored belief or an old story? In those moments, you may have believed you were moving forward yet never realized you were still anchored to heavy old energy, not allowing you to truly move forward. If that belief is anchored in L1 energy, it does not matter what you try or who offers to help you, you will remain stuck until you actually release the anchor and allow your energy to shift into a higher LOE.

Is your boat anchored in the old you, the old traumas, the old anger? Is that anchor so deeply embedded in the muck it would take a hundred people to pull it out? Is it committing you to a story that keeps repeating? Take a moment and embrace how the anchor sank and acknowledge that even though it may take a hundred people to pull the anchor out, it only takes one intentional and ready person to cut the line. One single person. Release the anchor. Release the old story and release the belief it built around you. You are moving on. Snip the line and allow it to sink. Allow it to sink so far into the bottom of the ocean that it can never again cause another person pain.

Acknowledge it. Validate it. And release it. You have all the tools you need to move forward. Release the anchor. Float away. And be free.

Only look back once you are far enough away that you can happily wave goodbye. Allow the emotions that come with the release. Enjoy the sea as you allow the grief, the sadness or whatever emotion wants to come up and out. Allow it. Release it. Allow it again. And release it again. This is how we heal.

If you activate something without resistance, it moves faster.

Questions for Insight

➤ What is the biggest anchor you have uncovered thus far?

➢ How does that anchor serve you?

_____

_____

_____

_____

➢ What beliefs have you built around that anchor?

_____

_____

_____

_____

➢ What do you need to believe in order to
cut the line?

_____

_____

_____

_____

➤ What is possible once you cut the line?

➤ How will you know that you are ready to
cut the line?

➤ What will never be possible if you consciously
decide to hold onto the burdening anchor?

➢ Are you ok with that last answer?

_____

_____

_____

_____

_____

➢ What action will you take next?

_____

_____

_____

_____

_____

_____

_____

_____

_____

_____

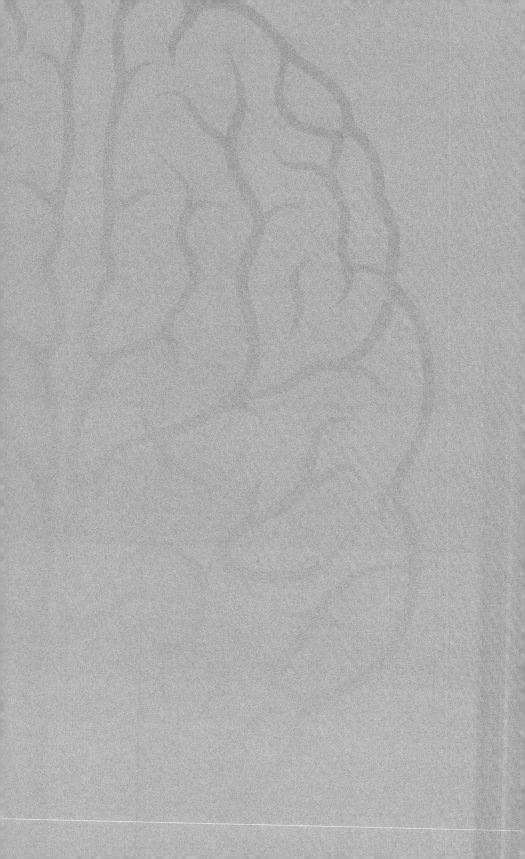

Chapter 11

Powerful Stories We Tell Ourselves

Powerful Stories We Tell Ourselves was actually the title of my first book. However, as I started to write that book, I realized I had yet to establish the presence of the map, the place where the stories reside. Having now established that foundation, this chapter is about the culmination of my life experiences, as well as the foundation to the biggest challenges that my clients unknowingly face—the stories. Stories like:

I'm bad at math.

I'm not smart enough to . . .

But then I'd have to start over.

I can't do that because . . .

I never finished college so I can't do . . .

I have kids so I can't . . .

My husband won't let me . . .

My wife won't let me . . .

I'm too tall for . . .

I'm too short for . . .

I'm too old to . . .

I don't have the money to . . .

and all the other powerful stories we tell ourselves.

These are just a glimpse of the myriad of stories you and I, and many others, have been reciting for decades. Whether the stories are told internally or verbally to others, over time we become convinced of their validity. The stories are a culmination of everything that's currently residing on each of our respective maps. Mine hosts my stories. Yours host your stories. And each person's map hosts their stories.

Your stories hold your beliefs, the new ones and the old ones. They hold all six of your layers. They hold your old values and your new ones. They hold the TEA you spill, the thoughts you emanate, the behaviors you experience and the LOE with which you experience them. They hold your achievements, your boundaries, your proudest moments, your saddest days, your biggest failures, your expectations, your default LOE, your limitations, your biggest secrets, the things that push you forward as well as all the things that hold you back. They also include your level of consciousness around the patterns, the countless anchors and all the triggers that engage your energy. That collection of energy that's deeply embedded into your map and houses all the things that you believe about you is your story.

It's these exact stories that keep you contracted in the spaces you attempt to expand into. They keep you captive in spaces where others feel freedom. These stories are merely an unconscious vice that keeps you safe. They protect you from trying things that might challenge your values, your beliefs, your thoughts, and your LOE. And the more you tell yourself these stories, they eventually create roadblocks that unconsciously keep you safe and prevent you from taking any further action. Remember that because your brain is simply trying to keep you alive and out of harm's way, it reads some of your deepest desires as *danger, danger* and stops you dead in your tracks, unable to move forward.

How Stories Work

What you've learned thus far is the more heightened your emotion, the deeper your anchors are set. Know that stories emerge from those moments. Those stories create thoughts. And as Louise Hay once shared, thoughts have no power over us unless we give it to them; they are simply words that are strung together.[33] Those thoughts only have power because you give them power. The moment that something occurs and shifts your LOE, either higher or lower than your default flow space, a story is created, often leaving behind a thought, an anchor and a new belief. Some typical examples would be:

I don't like taking that road because every time I drive down that road a deer jumps out in front of my car.

I don't like visiting that restaurant because their waitstaff is always rude, the food is cold, the place is dirty, etc.

I'd love to go back to school, but I can't because I don't have time.

I'd love to have kids, but I can't because I'm too old.

I'd like to move, but we have family here so I can't.

Although these moments may feel really simple and pretty harmless, these stories are actually the pivotal spaces that continually keep you stuck and unable to take action. You see, in the moments that you are looking to make a change or do something new, it's rare that you don't actually have the skill necessary to complete the task. It's often more that you haven't updated your story around that skill, task, relationship, etc. The stuck feeling comes when the old story and the new energy collide.

For instance, you have tons of confidence, yet every now and then you have a story that interrupts your ability to access confidence in the moment. Confidence is one of the main skills people ask me to help them build as a coach. I quickly remind them that they are already confident. Then they spend the next ten minutes confidently disagreeing with me. In those moments, I ask them how confident they are that they can spell their first and last name. They respond to me as if they've misheard me. I then ask if they are confident that they know where they live? Are they confident that they can recite the alphabet? Are they confident that they still know how to drive a car? Ride a bike? Walk and chew gum? The questions continue to get crazier, and the game persists until they realize that they are in fact pretty confident.

You see, we are all incredibly confident people; it's just in certain areas we are running old stories that interrupt our access to that amazing, brilliant confidence. You spend the majority of the day unknowingly confident in how to stay alive, how to feed yourself, how to work, play, bathe, shop, drive and walk. Know that it's not about confidence. It never was. It's about the story you're telling yourself in that moment that pauses your confidence. It's about learning what pattern you shift into in certain scenarios that pulls forward the story that pauses your confidence.

People often believe their thoughts run them rather than knowing you can change your thoughts by simply rewriting your story. You can create the thoughts that move you forward. The more you allow the stories to be told over and over again, the more you unconsciously convince yourself that they're true. The more you start to understand the origins of your stories and create conscious awareness around all the things they're connected to, the more you can start to dismantle them and find success. If the stories are not acknowledged and unpacked, that looped response will run until you interrupt it. Learning the loops and the stories that you are running and the outcomes they create around you is the foundation to sustainable change.

Understanding Anxiety

Although this may not be a popular opinion and may sound different from the current medical approach to anxiety, I believe that anxiety is a learned behavior. Much like the confidence loop, anxiety is another looped TEA pattern that emanates from a powerful story. If you are not someone who suffers from anxiety, take a moment and recognize how you process and release your emotions as they come up. If you are someone who suffers from anxiety, I invite you to go on a short journey with me.

Pause for a moment and imagine the very first time you ever had that anxious feeling. Take another moment and breathe. Close your eyes if you need to and allow yourself to go back to that very first time. I'm asking you to go back to the first time you had an anxious feeling, not your first anxiety attack. You are looking for the first time you experienced the feeling. If you can identify the first time that feeling came up and it made you uncomfortable, before the anxiety/panic attacks started, that's the moment you are looking for.

That moment you first experienced this feeling was probably a long time ago. And my guess is that your response to that feeling was much smaller than it is today. It was much smaller because, over time, you have unknowingly mastered this pattern, this loop. Today when this thought surfaces for you, the anxious feelings follow and the action/outcome intensifies.

Use the table below and identify what thought starts the looped response for you. The actions below are only a partial list of possible responses. Yours may greatly differ.

Your Story	Thought	Emotion	Action
What is the story you are telling yourself that creates the thought?	What thought starts this process for you?	Anxious	Intense breathing, shortness of breath, rapid heart rate, sweaty palms, disconnected, stuck, heavy, L1 energy

Note the similarities in your pattern and in the pattern provided. Notice the loop continues cycling through—thought, emotion, action, trigger, thought, emotion, action, trigger, over and over and over again. Even once the trigger is removed or no longer present, the loop can still repeat. Each time this cycle repeats itself, the process gets faster, more intense and a bit scarier. The picture gets larger. The sound gets louder. The feeling intensifies. The picture gets even larger. The sound gets a bit louder. The feeling intensifies again. Eventually, the whole process becomes paralyzing. Bigger. Louder. Faster. And faster. And before you know it, you feel completely out of control, often to the point that you may seek medical attention.

thought

**Anxiety Loop
TEA Model**

internal processing
KAVOG intake ·
remembering past event

coaching model

emotion

internal states
anchored memories
intensity, color, sound

©2022 by Jodee Gibson

trigger

action

internal or external

external response
behaviors · outcome
physical experience

This entire series of events began with a story—an old, anchored story that created a thought that threw you out of alignment, out of coherence and out of a LOE that you find manageable. Breathe. If that example heightened your anxious feelings, do the complete opposite and slow this pace down.

Make the picture in your mind just a bit smaller.

Breathe in for just a bit longer.

Exhale for a few more seconds.

Find something to focus on and begin making a
    new picture.

Generate a new feeling.

And intentionally step into that new story and away from
    that old process.

I share this example knowing that if you can speed up the pace and jump into an anxiety-ridden state by simply reading those few paragraphs above, then you are also capable of slowing it down by reading the text above and interrupting the story. Feelings are meant to be felt and released. If certain feelings stay for longer than necessary, take inventory of which layer they are attached to and begin to unpack that space of your map.

Anxiety is a looped, learned behavior that is mastered over time. It's mastered with minimal, if any, conscious awareness and begins with a story that generates a thought that leads to an anxious feeling. Because that anxious feeling does not sit well with you, the loop starts cycling. Identifying the story and the thought that starts this cycle and learning how it was originally encoded onto your map will lead you directly to the outcome you currently experience. The story you tell yourself determines the emotions you experience, and until you Interrupt the Story, you will continue experiencing these types of emotions and outcomes.

PAUSE WITH JODEE: If this feels insurmountable, you are 100 percent on the right track. If you are currently thinking *this feels hard or you don't know what you're talking about Jodee*, you are exactly the person I'm talking to. This exact, looped pattern that you're stuck in starts with a powerful story you unconsciously tell yourself. And from that story, a thought emerges that starts your TEA flowing. Know that it's simply a thought. What thought could you allow yourself to think that dramatically changes this action, outcome or behavior?

Identify the Story

In order to stop the thoughts, stop the physiological response and stop experiencing the undesirable outcomes, you must first identify the origin of the story. The continual action of re-experiencing that part of your map until it makes you viscerally respond only stops when you identify the layer it is attached to. Identifying and isolating the layer (root cause) creates the awareness needed to access the loop. And because the looped response has a chemical component, identifying and isolating this root cause will also allow you to recognize what level of energy it was originally encoded in. My guess is it's heavily catabolic.

Understanding those chemical responses is key in shifting the LOE. If the loop is layered in catabolic energy, your body is producing cortisol and adrenaline each and every time you retell the story and relive it. Catabolic energy is paralyzing. Creating conscious awareness and interrupting the story by introducing a new thought allows your body, at a minimum, to stop experiencing catabolic energy and, at a maximum, to start experiencing anabolic energy. Anabolic energy is expansive and saturates your brain with endorphins. The more anabolic energy you are intentionally producing the better outcomes you will experience. Healing begins with intentional action. Intentional, conscious awareness is necessary here.

Regardless of where you are in the loop, each time you Interrupt the Story and stop the loop from closing, your brain starts building a new neural pathway. Remember what you learned about neuroplasticity. Sustainable change is created by finding yourself in any part of the loop and stopping it from closing. Conscious awareness is the fastest way to change. Awareness equals access. The self-awareness that you will gain from identifying roots and unpacking stories is incredibly more powerful than ignoring the trigger and focusing on the person that engages it.

The more often you tell the story, the more powerful it becomes.

—BESSEL VAN DER KOLK

Take a moment and revisit your answers from chapter 10. Resonate on the triggers and the thoughts that engage your TEA patterns.

What story are the thoughts connected to?

If there were identifiable triggers, what anchored beliefs are they challenging, and what story are those anchors connected to?

How accurate and effective do you believe the story is today?

If you could rewrite the story now, what details would you change?

What would you add or remove?

What LOE would you shift it into?

If it's rooted in L1 (shame, blame, victim energy) or L2 (anger, aggression, hostility), are you really still a victim to something that happened so long ago?

What is the goal of the story?

Allow me to share something here. I often paused while writing this book thinking; *Who am I to be sharing this content?* And then I remember, I am the perfect person to share this content because it's my story too. Who better to share it than someone who was traumatized herself as a child and then spent three decades researching and learning every facet of human behavior in order to heal? I mastered equanimity long before I learned to spell the word. Know that this chapter and the one that follows are the heart of, not only this book, but also the heart of my life's work. I get choked up as I type these words, knowing, not only, how pivotal the content of these two chapters were for me, yet also how deeply rich in content they are and how powerful they were in my journey. I am hoping they can do the same for you. These next two chapters are life changing.

The paradigm shifts that occurred for me from this content alone completely changed the trajectory of my life. It was Korzybski's six words—*the map is not the territory*—that pulled it all together for me. At that moment I realized I was living in a story that I did not write. It was a story that had been written around me by a map that was created *for* me, not *by* me. And I was navigating the territory with that incredibly outdated, ineffective map. The culmination of your layered map creates the storyline that you live inside today.

Your story is the culmination of everywhere you have ever been leading up to this moment. Your map and your story include all the things you personally deem as possible and impossible. It's about understanding that your story navigates the direction of your journey. These stories, regardless of validity, create your future. They create your kids' futures, your clients' futures, and the futures of all the people around you. Yet the question remains, how true is the story?

Each thought you think emanates from your story. This story of yours is powerful; it's either powerfully keeping you out of a success pattern or it's powerfully leading you toward your desired goal. Know this to be true: It does not matter what the stories may sound like now, or who the authors may have been, the story is editable. Creating awareness around the stories and the limitations they create around you is step one in rewriting them. And regardless of the depths of muck you may imagine yourself to be burdened in now, know that lotus flowers grow from the darkest and murkiest of places. Your story was given to you for a reason. Anything is possible from exactly where you are now.

No mud. No lotus.

—THICH NHAT HANH[34]

No one else on this planet can change your story or remove the muddy waters. You simply get to decide how powerful these stories are and if and how they are serving you. Take a moment and reflect on all the notes you've taken thus far. What is the culmination of the story or stories you are telling yourself?

Using the information provided in chapter 9, what's truly the default LOE that your stories and your responses self-level? I'm asking you to be really honest in finding that answer. Oftentimes we look at the chart and go to the highest level of energy that we've ever felt. In this scenario, I'm asking you to look at the chart and put your finger on the first LOE that comes up when that first memory comes up. The more honest you are with yourself, the more sustainable change you will experience. Looking at the breakdown in chapter 10, *section*

Finding Anchors, what LOE do the thoughts your TEA flows from align with?

> **PAUSE WITH JODEE:** These questions are not about judgment. They are about creating self-awareness. The more awareness you have, the more access you get to you. Without access, you will simply continue circling.

The Truth of the Story

All thoughts emanate from a story. The story you live inside. The story that your map has created over the course of your lifetime. The TEA model is an incredible tool, yet it's only effective if the thought you are building the mode on is actually true. By true, I mean big *T* truth. Big *T* truth means it's a universal truth, and regardless of who you asked, they would agree there was truth in what you shared. Little *t* truth means it's only true for you. Effective TEA models only work with big *T* truths.

If I, as your coach, allow you to start the TEA coaching process with a little *t* (un)true thought, I'm co-signing for the thought that you are basing all of your work on. The emotions and actions that follow are dependent on the initial *T*. How much different would your action or behavior be if it started with a big *T* truth carrying thought?

Big *T* Truth vs little *t* true

Big *T* Truth	little *t* true
I own a car.	I own an awesome car .
I live in a city.	I live in the best city.
I own a house.	I own an amazing house.
Everyone would agree.	*Everyone may not agree.*

....

Big *T* Truth	little *t* true
I am a mom/wife/leader/boss.	I am a bad mom/wife/leader/boss.
I speak Spanish.	I speak terrible Spanish.
I am an athlete.	I am a competitive athlete.
I am an employee.	I am the best/worst employee.
Everyone would agree.	*Everyone may not agree.*

©2022 by Jodee Gibson

The TEA model is built on the foundation of your thought. My extensive experience knows that the model works best with big *T* truths. Knowing that, using only the TEA model can sometimes stump you or blur the growth potential. If you are attempting to reach your goal, and you have a thought like *it's not going to work*, odds are high the emotion and action that emanates from that thought are way less powerful than the results that might come from a thought like *I'm scared as hell, but I'm going to trust the process.* Trust in the process versus stepping into something assuming that's not going to work provides two massively different outcomes.

Conscious Stories

By this point, I'm certain you have uncovered some really cool stuff about your map and now about your stories. You are embracing the idea that it's not about how people *make you feel*, it's about the story you start telling yourself when they start talking. It's about the feeling and the LOE that emanates from inside you when their words start flowing. The more times you tell it, the deeper it embeds itself onto your map. Regardless of the truth, or lack of truth, in the story, the more times you tell your story, the further you validate it. The more you validate it, the more proof you look for in the world. Eventually, you begin to build stories on top of those initial stories.

If you have decided you're bad at school, that story now serves as an anchor keeping you outside of an ideal career you may want. That story may keep you outside of different extracurricular activities you would need that skill for, yet you don't engage because *you're bad at science*. This rippled, trickle-down effect continues to permeate your map, layer-by-layer, invading and embedding itself into each and every layer it can access. It literally keeps you outside of your actual happiness because of that one rooted story. Imagine how many stories you have anchored down that probably are not as accurate as you remember them to be.

Take a moment and jot them down. What stories come to mind that you believe have strong roots or that you would like to challenge?

PAUSE WITH JODEE: If nothing is coming up for you, reverse engineer it. What life goals would you like to, or would have liked to, accomplish if that barrier simply was not there? Unpack the barrier and find the root. Stay with it. Meditate on it. Release it and allow it to flow. The answer will surface. Journal around it until you find the root. Know that this may take time. Odds are high the story is decades old and firmly anchored into your map and feels completely normal for you.

Challenge the Story

You have hundreds of loops running on a daily basis that create freedom for you. They give you freedom from having to manage several different redundant tasks your brain would rather simplify and create a loop for. These loops run unconsciously and free from your input. They run without your knowledge and without your need for guidance. My biggest challenge with our Western view of the world is that we continually attempt to change behaviors, oftentimes medicating them, without ever investigating the pattern that creates them. Behaviors are the expression of a problem, not the actual problem.

Behaviors run in that same looped response pattern and will continue to cycle through the loop until interrupted or intentionally stopped. Uninterrupted, the loop will cycle over and over and over again, normalizing not only the behavior but each step of the loop as well. Your loops run on default. There are multiple steps and decisions involved in a loop. These loops are founded in your story, which your values, your beliefs, your thoughts, your emotions and your actions emanate from. Uncovering those steps, creating awareness around the decisions made with them, and then identifying what merged them together is an integral part of affecting sustainable change.

Is it really true that you're bad at math? Or did you simply have a paralyzing experience—somewhere between the ages of eight and twelve—that hijacked your neurology and dropped a heavy anchor. It paralyzed you to the point that you just stopped taking in information. It's not that you're bad at math, it's that whoever was teaching you math in that moment didn't understand the way your brain needed to learn it. It's not that you're bad at math, it's that the teacher you had used paralyzing words that were then forever embedded onto your map.

As a child of that age, know that you trusted your teacher and were willingly expanded, wide-open, ready to learn. When that anchor dropped, because you were so wide-open, it fell deep to the bottom, and it was firmly anchored in your brain. Math is all around us, from gas prices, to how many hours a week we work, to how much money an hour we make, to our rent, our mortgage, our bills, to our extracurricular activities, to every time we run to the store. My guess is that you're pretty good with numbers. Maybe you want to be better at them, but you're definitely not bad at them. The story you have attached to them still feels true because the anchor is so deep.

The best way to unpack a story or to challenge an event is to think back to that moment. Take a deep breath, close your eyes and think back to that time and space. When you reflect, ask yourself the following questions and allow whatever comes up to surface.

Where were you physically, and who was around you?

Whose voice did you hear?

What is the tone of their voice telling you today?

What emotion (LOE) is bubbling up inside of you?

If you could tell your then-year-old self something right now from your today perspective that would ease that LOE, what would you say?

Knowing what you know now, what can you share with this younger version of you about the tone of voice the younger you anchored?

What did the younger you need to believe in that moment? How can you convey that to them now?

Chapter 12

Interrupt the Story™

O nce you decide to slow down and become aware, the stories just repeat and eventually become a part of your map. The more they run, the more they create a life of their own. The original root of the story sprouts out and invades your map, overtaking areas you never would have imagined could be connected to that initial event, running the same story. That story builds a pattern that starts running on a loop. That story creates a pattern, the pattern feeds the TEA, and the result validates the story, further anchoring the looped behavior. This loop runs until you stop it. This aligns with Bessel van der Kolk's thought that the more often you tell the story, the more powerful it becomes.[35] Dr. Bandler further concludes that the more you repeat the pattern, the more intense it gets until it eventually creates a physiological response.[36]

Change is Quicker Than You Think

Remember back when you were a child and you believed the stories your parents told you? Their stories led you to believe in fairy tales, the tooth fairy, and maybe even Santa Claus. You were fully bought in, as the stories seemed valid. Those stories weren't ideas you gradually had to get over and decide to change your beliefs around. You simply figured out one day that fairy tales are fairy tales and that the tooth fairy and Santa Claus were different than they had originally been described. In that moment everything changed. It wasn't a long, drawn-out process. You learned these things were not true, and you immediately shifted your beliefs and your story. In the moments of your life when change feels a bit more challenging than the example used above, know that you can always STOP and Interrupt the Story™.

Interrupt the Story

The quickest way to evoke change is to Interrupt the Story. The next time you find yourself inside a story that no longer serves you or is not going to increase your ability to accomplish your ideal outcome, I invite you to STOP. Take a moment and STOP the story. From the edge of the story, answer the following questions.

Interrupt the Story™

S	Story **serve**	Create conscious awareness around your story. *How does this story serve you?*
T	Truth **true**	Does this story have universal truth in it? *Is this story only true for you?*
O	Options **opportunities**	What options are available when you stay committed to this story? *What opportunities appear when you release it?*
P	Power **possibilities**	What happens to your power when you stay inside this story? *What is actually possible outside this story?*

©2022 by Jodee Gibson

Gain the clarity that comes from investigating these questions and getting incredibly clear on what keeps them alive. Interrupting the story and gaining conscious awareness around each piece of that foundational space is literally life changing. It's in these spaces that you begin to realize what's on your map and how long it's been there. Allow yourself the time and space to STOP and ask the appropriate questions. Repeat this process each and every time you find yourself in a familiar pattern, in a familiar story or in a space that simply feels stuck. Your map is laden with story after story after story, each of which holds powerful beliefs for you. Rarely, if ever, do you stop and disassemble the story in this manner. Get deep into the trenches and understand the foundational parts of your map that allow you to intentionally recalibrate your position. Also understand that when you Interrupt the Story and you STOP, it allows you to later revisit the TEA method with a clear, big *T* thought.

The Foundation of a Story

Recall any of the stories and analogies that have been shared thus far. Whether it was the afraid of dogs scenario, the artist scene from Part I, any of the other dozens that were shared or a story of your own you have uncovered from reading this book, each time you replay that story, a series of pictures or a movie of that memory replays in your head. Your memory of these stories has now become an actual movie in your mind. Much like an anxiety attack, each time you recall the picture in your head, you add color, you add sound, you add intensity, you add emotion and you add volume. The screen gets bigger and the picture becomes a movie, and it runs at a faster pace each time you unconsciously recall it. In the present day, all you have to do is recall the video—that you unconsciously made all by yourself—and you are immediately in a full-blown anxiety attack.

Of course it feels extraordinarily overwhelming! You're gasping for air because this video has hijacked every single piece of your nervous system with its recalled KAVOG triggers, all of which are highly intensified, and it all feels wildly out of control. So it makes complete sense that reaching for a vice or a medication that can turn down that out of control, over-stimulated, incredibly intense movie sounds like a great idea. Yet knowing what you know now, how sustainable is that approach?

I invite you to sit down with your dog engagement memory, your I'm afraid of water story, your I'm afraid of elevators or spiders story, your I'm bad at math story, or any other story you have created in your mind. Sit down and Interrupt the Story. Walk yourself through the story. Identify each step, each piece, and get in the weeds with your insight. Become aware of the stories you are telling yourself and unpack those spaces like never before. The next few paragraphs briefly walk you through my Dissociated Healing™ model.

Take yourself back to the moment you remember that story running for the first time and unpack each and every piece of it. Get crystal clear on the foundation of it. Know who was present while that story was being created. Understand the emotional response you would have had access to at that age. Take a moment and acknowledge who you were in that moment. Understand where that version of you felt safe and take your current self there. Disassociate from that version of you and allow there to be two of you, the original-aged version of you in the memory and the present-day you.

If you were five years old when that event took place, where did you feel the safest when you were five? Was it on your front porch? Was it in your bedroom closet? Was it in the backyard on your swing set? Was it at school? Wherever you felt the safest, take that then-aged version of yourself to that space and have a conversation. Allow five-year-old you to know that you're in charge now, and that it's ok to have strong emotions from that event yet share that you're going to keep you safe from now on. Share that it's ok to release the memory and the fear because you are going to take it from here. Share with that five-year-old that they don't need to protect you. Maybe you were thirteen in that memory. Share with your thirteen-year-old self what you know now, as your today-year-old self, on how to heal.

You can only start from where you are. Honor the things that come up. Understand what the story was about and understand what you are making it mean today. This is how we heal, by interrupting the stories and building new intentionally healthy, foundational spaces to function from. Odds are high that the most impactful stories that lead you arrived on your map well before the age of eight years old.

You can only start from where you are.
Honor the things that come up.

When you change the way you think about things, it changes the way you feel. If you don't like the feelings you're having, change the thoughts and the stories that create them. This is not a psychological shift, rather a physiological and neurological one. If thoughts create our emotions, then let's think about the emotions we want and reverse engineer the process. Create the ideal emotion, and then map out what you need to believe in order to provoke that emotion. This is about thinking instead of remembering. Allow me to share that I am beyond obsessed with yoga and have been practicing for decades. Holding onto an emotion is like holding a yoga pose until you can't hold it any longer and then holding it some more.

Think about the pain. The discomfort. The burning sensation. The inability to focus on anything else but the pain. You cannot absorb love. You cannot absorb kindness. You literally cannot think about anything around you except the pain. You cannot function or focus on anything else until you release.

How much sense does that make? Being contracted and holding onto an emotion is damaging. And in these moments, you are most likely looking for an external solution to an internal struggle. Know that change starts internally. Acknowledge the story. Release the pain. Protecting your foundation is imperative. This reminds me of one of Dr. Bandler's analogies: Imagine what would happen if the gutters on your home were rerouted and fed back into your basement windows, or into the crawl space beneath your house instead of draining properly and allowing the water to flow away from your foundation. How long would it take before your foundation started to fail? Emotions work much the same. Continuing to allow the looped patterns to run on an infinite cycle does not provide an end, nor is it sustainable. Acknowledging the emotions, understanding their origins, validating the story they have created over time and then releasing it is how you heal.

Listen, I know this chapter was packed full, yet each individual piece here inevitably links together. Learning them together and understanding them together is fundamental to your continual use of them later. Understanding your story, embracing the TEA model, and having the capacity to Interrupt the Story are the three main components to creating sustainable change.

Masking the Pain

When we choose to remain in the old story and instead just mask the pain, this is simply another vice. Whether it's masked through consuming alcohol, drugs or too much food; too much or too little exercise; living on cigarettes, coffee or energy drinks; or whatever your vice of choice is, it's all masking the same pain, and it all leads back to your same old story. A story that allows you to hide. A story that allows you to create a facade. A story that allows you to protect yourself from the pain you feel yet cannot unpack just yet.

Wearing every single dollar you make and decorating your exterior with expensive jewelry, expensive clothes, the newest car, the best shoes and the five-figure watch all highlight your exterior, unconsciously or intentionally masking your interior. Decorating your exterior is about you, my friend; it's not about anybody around you. It's about you hiding everything underneath the watch, underneath the shoes, underneath the clothes, underneath the rings, the makeup, the hair, the nails, the muscles and the big house. Again, buying expensive stuff doesn't upgrade your internal programming; it simply masks the LOE you are experiencing and then attracts back to you more people that mask their pain.

When you have unconditional love,
conditional things no longer play
a role in your life.
—RINPOCHE

Although your mask protects you, the person you are hiding under the mask is still alive in there. The only people that are impressed by your masking are other people that wear masks. Your pain still emits a LOE that attracts matching energy—and energy self-levels. Know that you can heal that human. You can release and heal that story. Remember the embroidering story from chapter 2? Everyone's inside is messy. Embrace the mess. Discover the roots. Identify the LOE they were originally rooted in and then release the energy so you can rewrite the story. Doing this invites acceptance and maturation of that journey and eventually releases the need to mask it. I shared with you early that humor was always my favorite mask. Humor protected me in the darkest of days and in the most challenging times.

Think about it.

What is your fancy car masking?

What do your clothes mask?

What is your make-up masking?

What is your humor masking?

What does being so busy all the time mask?

What does your lifestyle mask for you?

What could you allow yourself to believe that releases the need for the mask?

This may be challenging to acknowledge, but are the people in your life attracted to the things you have externally or to the person you wholeheartedly are internally?

This is the exact reason I do not believe in continually repeating blanket affirmations. I do, however, believe in intentional, personally created affirmations. I can slap stickers all over the outside of my body demanding change, yet it doesn't change what's going on inside my body. Unless your affirmations speak directly to your limiting beliefs, they are pointless.

If you continually say *I am wealthy, I am wealthy, I am wealthy*, but you don't understand how your finances work, odds are high you will not end up wealthy. If you instead say *I am worthy of learning how money works,* or *I am worthy of understanding my finances*, those affirmations will take you much further than just stating *I am wealthy*. I masked with humor to deflect away from my disastrous inside. The *I am wealthy* statement does the same; it's simply masking your internal story yet never addresses the roots.

If somebody makes you feel unwelcome, know that unwelcoming energy was present in both of you well before the scenario unfolded. Something about your story, your LOE and your map drew them in. If somebody makes you feel unloved or neglected, that energy was present inside you long before that person even stepped in the room. If an event leaves you feeling anxious, know the anxiety was present before that event took place. I've said it before and I'll say it again: water self-levels and so does energy.

Water self-levels and so does energy.

The reason you keep ending up with the same result is because your waterline of energy determines the experiences you attract. If you're triggered, understand the anchor belongs to you, and it was there long before someone's words engaged it. If your feelings are hurt, that wound was open long before they arrived. Remember TEA: the way you feel is in direct correlation to your thoughts. Your thoughts emanate from your story. Until you Interrupt the Story, unwanted TEA will continue to flow. If you want to feel better, you have to think differently.

Ego versus Soul

When you stop trying to fix the world or mask yourself and instead start healing your energy and healing your internal juxtaposed story, it's only then that you begin to release the enmeshed people and trauma from your story. When you understand your story and the players in it, you begin to find grace and hold space for others, free from judgment, with complete curiosity, detached from any involvement. You start to move away from ego and start to operate from a soulful place. From that space, your energy shifts, your story changes, your TEA starts flowing differently and the waterline rises. From that space, you attract a completely different collection of energies.

Again, do you want to live a full ninety years, or do you want to live the same year ninety times?[37] With the new awareness you have around your map, it now becomes a choice. It's a choice because you now have all the tools you need in order to make the changes necessary. It's now just a choice as to if and when you will implement them. It's not that you don't know what's keeping you back. You learned that in the previous chapters. Check your answers at the end of each chapter. When you begin to peel back the layers and you embrace the idea that it's all just a story, you gain access and personal power like you've never had before.

Story Takeaways

- ➢ If you're going to make up a story about yourself, make it fun, make it exciting, make yourself the hero and make sure it's one that increases your LOE.

- ➢ If you're telling an old story about someone else that's laden in catabolic energy, that lowers your LOE too. Who does that really serve?

- ➢ Once you value yourself, your LOE rises and you attract others that will value you too.

- ➢ Create powerful boundaries for yourself and demand the same.

- ➢ Interrupt the Story as often as possible.

- ➢ Stay conscious of your masks and the powerful stories you create around them.

- ➢ If you are contracted, you are responding unconsciously with a lower level of energy (shame, blame, anger, sympathy).

- ➢ If you are expanded, you are responding consciously with a higher level of energy (curiosity, empathy, optimism).

- ➢ You are an amazing, beautiful soul that is worthy of writing a new story.

Chapter 13

Trauma, Emotional Development & Arrested Emotional Development

Disclaimer: Some of the content in this chapter may be triggering. As you learn this content and take it all in, it may evoke old anchors, memories and triggers. This entire book is about creating awareness. It is not about blaming or judgment. If and when you find yourself in shame, blame or judgment, STOP and Interrupt the Story. Process the emotions that come up. Allow them to flow and then release them. Take a moment, breathe and find your center, and then continue on. Repeat this process as often as possible.

In keeping with the rest of the book, this content will be delivered in as close to laymen's terms as possible. I will also make my best effort to snorkel versus scuba dive, but there may be times that scuba diving is necessary.

As you dive into this chapter, know that it is the pinnacle of my life's work . . . thus far. I have written all the previous pages to get to this point. This is the last piece to the puzzle that I had unknowingly yet desperately been searching for. You may unknowingly be searching for the same. I vividly remember the exact moment I stumbled across Dr. Paul Hegstrom's book *Broken Children, Grown Up Pain*. I felt like it took a lifetime to read, not because it was long or confusing, more so because it spoke directly to my soul. It evoked awareness in me and opened doors I never knew existed. It answered the questions I had yet to ask, never realizing there could be an answer so clear. I remember reading a few pages and then having to put the book down and process what I had just read. His work took me deep into the trenches of my own childhood and cathartically uncovered the concept of arrested emotional development.

As I read each and every page, his acknowledgment validated my journey. It explained in great detail what happens when people experience trauma early. It validated what I had normalized. This chapter is a culmination of his book along with the work of many other developmental psychology masters. It covers emotional development, emotional regulation, emotional dysregulation, trauma and arrested emotional development. Essentially, it's about developmental trauma and the evidence it leaves in its wake. The clarity you will gain from this content is life changing.[38]

Thus far you have learned about all six of your layers, your patterns, your boundaries, your anchors, your triggers, your LOE and most importantly, the stories you tell yourself around it all. We've talked about your childhood, your past traumas and your ability to become consciously aware of the unconscious patterns that create your reality. You have learned how your life has created each respective piece and how they all come together on your map. This chapter adds depth to all of that content.

In these next pages, you will learn more precisely how each one of these layers landed on your map and how they are currently functioning. You will learn how to recognize the things that no longer serve you, how to process them and how to remove them from your map. This content has the capacity to immediately shift everything you have ever known about yourself, your life and the people you surround yourself with. This is the belly of healthy, conscious, sustainable healing.

Emotional Development

Emotional development is the path you take as a child when learning what emotions are, understanding how to feel your feelings, how to process your feelings and how to release your feelings. You are born with the innate desire to connect and attach. As a baby, you cried initially because of your discomfort, yet you were unconsciously also seeking connection and attachment. The combination of reducing what engaged the discomfort (hunger, dirty diaper, need for connection) and engaging in human connection is what soothed you. Once both needs were met and your physiology was soothed, you shifted back into coherence. As you grew, the process repeated and built a behavioral pattern. Eventually, the sight of someone coming towards you to your aid automatically and prematurely soothed you because your neurology knew the familiar pattern.

By the age of two or three, you had the capacity to feel your feelings, yet you did not have the words to express them. This may have left you frustrated and unable to establish healthy communication. In those moments, someone may have witnessed you throwing a tantrum in an attempt to express all of the new and very overwhelming emotions you were feeling. Those new feelings overtook your previously calm state, similar to an L7 energy, and left you feeling L1 emotions. Imagine the intensity at which your feelings were magnified. Not only were they new feelings, yet at two or three years old, you did not have the capacity or the vocabulary to articulate what you were trying to process. Much like soothing a crying newborn, the presence of an emotionally regulated adult helped you, the toddler, learn how to feel your feelings and how to process your emotions. This created not only the space for you to develop a secure, healthy attachment but also taught you how to emotionally self-regulate. If an adult was not present or you were not able to learn how to process your emotions, see the section on emotional dysregulation.

Bessel van der Kolk said, "Associating intense sensations with safety, comfort, and mastery is the foundation of self-regulation, self-soothing, and self-nurture . . . a secure attachment combined with the cultivation of competency builds an *internal locus of control*, the key factor in healthy coping."[39] This is a two-fold area, secure attachment and emotional regulation. Not only are you, as a baby or toddler, learning that feeling feelings is safe and that processing feelings is safe, yet you are also learning what it feels like to develop a secure, healthy attachment while doing so, which establishes the foundations you will forever build upon for secure connection. Connection is what regulates you.[40]

A second fundamental piece of emotional development is consistency. When you grow up in a consistently safe environment, your ability to form secure attachments and develop secure connections becomes second nature. Regardless of whether the consistency is delivered by one parent or two, a grandparent, a family member, a foster parent, a teacher or a coach, whoever that consistent force is for you as a child determines your ability to develop secure connections. Lack of that consistency invites the lack of secure attachment, leaving you predisposed later in life to emotional dysregulation.[41]

Whichever one of these was present for you as a child is the one that you have normalized. It's also possible that you developed in an environment that was either inconsistent or had two parents that offered different things. One may have protected you, created a secure attachment, allowing you to emotionally develop and self-regulate, while the other may have done the exact opposite. The latter kept you on guard.

Between the ages of three and five, you moved into the space of learning to manage your emotions, provided you had the opportunity to develop healthy, secure attachments and build secure connections. It's at this stage you developed sympathy and began to understand the emotions you were feeling were not universally felt. You learned that even though you were feeling sad, everyone else in the world may not have been feeling sad at that moment. Acknowledging and validating those feelings became essential to understanding and embracing the idea that having strong emotions and feeling your feelings was normal and safe.

When that acknowledgement and validation is missing in this stage of life, you may begin to isolate and hide your feelings. It's in this stage that shame emerges and often gets anchored onto your map. Because you are experiencing huge emotions and no one is ready, willing or able to validate your experience or help guide you through the journey, the initial emotion gets anchored along with feelings of abandonment and shame, creating a deep wound on your map.

Emotional Regulation

By the age of five to six, if and when you've had the capacity to thrive in an emotionally healthy environment with care-takers who engage appropriately, that experience creates a solid foundation for emotional regulation to build upon. At this point, you will be fluent in acknowledging your feelings, understanding their impact and having the ability to process them in a healthy, constructive way. This emotional regulation creates the foundation for building future healthy relation-ships with others as well as with yourself. Emotional regu-lation includes building boundaries, having an awareness of your triggers and understanding and engaging in your self-care. Once you are emotionally regulated, empathy and com-passion begin to emerge.

Understand that in no way, shape or form am I saying that as a six-year-old child you had the capacity to process adult emotions. I'm simply creating awareness that by the age of six, you have established a solid foundation for emotional regulation and the ability to self-regulate to further expand. By the age of six, you have the awareness to know when a strong emotion is coming up and that you are allowed to feel that intense emotion. You have an awareness of what triggers those emotions—you're afraid of the dark, afraid of strangers, anxious to meet new friends, sad to end a play date or resis-tant to bedtime.

These are all things that may heighten your emotions, yet when you are aware of them and understand how emotions work, you have the ability and skills to process them in a healthy way. Even though it's often with adult supervision at that age, you understand the importance of and are able to engage in self-care activities, such as brushing your teeth, washing your face, taking a bath, cleaning up behind yourself, picking up your toys or honoring your bedtime; and you can engage those activities independently, while managing the emotions that come with them. It's in this space that you learn to build trust.

Four Universal Needs

From the experiences listed above, your four universal needs emerge. Although you have a multitude of needs, the four universal needs that are key to building a sustainable foundation for emotional regulation are belonging, mastery, independence and generosity. The presence of these four needs also plays a pivotal role in building your values and other layers as well.

Belonging generates the feelings of being welcomed, wanted and loved. Without this, you are left feeling neglected, unwanted, left out and left behind.

Mastery is having the capacity to try things over and over again with a supportive adult encouraging you. The more you try, the better you get. Without this need being met, you may feel as if you do not have much to offer the world or even yourself.

Independence is having a strong sense of self and your ability to create internal cadence. When you do not have access to this, you are not able to access your personal power and are left feeling L1 energy (powerless, helpless, victim energy), waiting for someone to come fix it.

Generosity creates the feeling that you have something to offer, something of value that you can share with others. Without the ability to contribute, you may be left feeling a lack of worth.[42]

People rise to the environment you build around them.

The presence of each of these four universal needs is not only necessary yet imperative for healthy emotional regulation. When present, these four universal needs leave you in coherence and provide a secure, balanced sense of self. When one of these four universal needs is missing, the hole it leaves for you as a child and the open wound it places on your map creates a layer where you are left out of balance, distorted or dysregulated. The position this creates leaves you unable to cope. What causes the imbalance, distortion or dysregulation is the presence of trauma. Your map collects and houses each one of your traumas.[43]

What Is Trauma?

As shared in chapter 1, trauma is the emotional and physiological response you experience to a deeply disturbing event. Trauma is truly anything that takes you out of your coherent state or outside of your ability to create coherence and into a fight or flight response. Trauma is any action or event that leaves you outside of your four universal human needs. It's any event that leaves you outside of your ability to emotionally regulate, with or without the presence of a trusted adult. As Gabor Maté often shares, trauma is not what happened to you; trauma is what happens *inside* you due to the things that happened to you. Regardless of how big or small the event was or how often it occurred, that event created a physiological response, built a belief and anchored it to your map. The more the same pattern of trauma occurs, the deeper the anchor sets, the more embedded the belief becomes and the more you normalize it as healthy behavior.[44]

Trauma is an inevitable part of our lives. I share that in hopes of enlightening everyone that trauma is all around us. The more we recognize it and process it, the healthier we become. The more we ignore it, hold on to it and overlook the effects it's having on our physiology, the more damaging it becomes and the more it pervades into many other areas of our lives. Learning to process trauma and learning healthy coping skills is an essential part of life. Building resilience can be a powerful tool, yet processing the trauma is still necessary. Most people simply normalize the pain, internalize the effects it had on them and carry on, never realizing the emotional weight they are carrying.[45]

How much trauma are we normalizing and allowing in, simply because we do not know any better? Although addressing the trauma, feeling it and acknowledging it, may seem insurmountable, carrying it around with you for the next twenty to forty years is way more painful. Sometimes doing the right thing is the most painful option, yet it creates the most freedom. Release the anchor. Dismantle the trigger. Allow the wound to heal. You will continue acting out the trauma until you release it.

Pause for a moment and jot down what's coming up for you. Create conscious awareness around it by making a note of:

When I'm feeling worthy I _____

When I'm feeling unworthy I _____

When I feel_____, it brings back the feeling of_____

When I hear_____, it brings back the feeling of _____

When I see_____, it brings back the feeling of _____

When I taste_____, it brings back the feeling of _____

When I smell_____, it brings back the feeling of _____

Create massive consciousness around your patterns. Know what happens in your body when those thoughts come to mind. Consciously map out your physiology. Use this space as overflow for the previous activity or as needed.

Types of Trauma

Trauma is often divided into a few different categories, depending on how extreme the situation is. It baffles me that developmental trauma is still not recognized by the

American Psychiatric Association (APA), nor is it listed in the *Diagnostic and Statistical Manual of Mental Disorders* (DSM). Developmental trauma is the leading cause of so many of the mental health challenges that people attempt to manage, yet it's not recognized by the same people who write the prescriptions. The best breakdown at the moment is categorized as type 1, type 2 and type 3 trauma.[46]

Type 1: Single Exposure	Solid secure attachment established. Single exposure to trauma (i.e., house fire, loss of a parent, bullying episode, moving to a new house). This one, single event had a traumatic effect and the victim recovered.
Type 2: Multiple Exposures	One type of trauma, exposed multiple times or exposure to one to two different traumas in an inconsistent manner that may include neglect (emotionally and physically), bullying, physical assault, child abuse, domestic violence, divorce, parents in conflict, etc. The victim of type 2 trauma can articulate the exposure and the timeframe in which it occurred.
Type 3: Ongoing Toxic Stress	Multiple ongoing exposures that become "normal" for the victims. Victims do not know if/when their utilities will be disconnected, if/when their parents will be home, if/when food will be available to eat, no one available to emotionally connect with and they stay on edge awaiting further abuse, neglect, rejection, bullying, and/or incest/molestation often at the hand of family members. This is not one isolated event, but rather the person living in survival mode.[47] *If developmental trauma were recognized, it would fall into this category.*

A newly emerging fourth type of trauma is often referred to as a microtrauma. Microtraumas are the tiny, little yet consistent jabs which are definitely felt but weren't big enough to acknowledge—gas lighting, snide remarks, backhanded compliments, subtle verbal abuse, dismissal of the need to connect or the need to attach. This type of intentional, ma-nipulative trauma slowly eats away at your self-worth. It's the space where you know it occurred and you know there was a level of intent behind it that made you feel uncomfortable, yet it felt more uncomfortable to call the person out for such a small, subtle detail.

All of these traumas, regardless of how big or small, be-come layered into your map. These traumas not only impact your ability to thrive, yet they also have the capacity to com-pletely interrupt your emotional growth, at best delaying your ability to emotionally regulate. They also impact your ability to further emotionally develop.

With a type 1 trauma, your emotional development and your ability to self-regulate are both still present, provided you previously were emotionally regulated and have a se-cure attachment. Your ability to recover and move forward in life with minimal impact to your emotional development is very possible.

With a type 2 trauma, your emotional development be-comes stunted, dependent upon the consistency and depth of the multiple exposures in the area in which the trauma oc-curred. Your ability to self-regulate becomes strained even if you have a secure attachment. You can access some emotion-al regulation in certain areas while others will be challenging. In the absence of a secure attachment, it is common that you begin to self-soothe leading up to the trauma, during the trau-ma and after. Your LOE is L3.

With a type 3 trauma, your emotional development seizes, and you are, from that point forward, arrested in emotional development. Your ability to emotionally develop has been interrupted, and you are now emotionally dysregulated. You begin to expect and predict the abuse and trauma and your LOE is L1. Until the trauma is acknowledged, validated and released you will continue to self-soothe, most often with unhealthy vices—rocking, nail-biting, avoiding, substance abuse, emotional eating, detaching, people pleasing, etc.[48]

In the event that a secure adult was not present (attachment) and your needs were not met (self-regulation), or this connection was intermittent, odds are high you learned unhealthy ways to self-soothe. Those unhealthy patterns paired with the lack of connection later lead to emotional dysregulation.[49]

Emotional Dysregulation

Trauma isn't about the actual event. It's about how that event now shows up on your map and how your body responds to it. Does it expand, or does it contract? The presence of unprocessed trauma can be all pervading. Trauma robs you of the feeling that you are in charge of yourself; and what has happened cannot be undone, but what can be dealt with are the imprints of the trauma on the body, mind and soul, as Bessell shared.[50]

As we discussed in chapter 7 from Morris Massey's work, if these imprints were created before the age of seven (the imprinting stage), your brain has accepted them as normal behavior and they may not stand out. If the trauma occurred between the ages of seven and fourteen (the modeling stage), you were expanded, ready to learn the world through modeling others and absorbed the behavior of the role models around you. If none of this stands out to you, you may have simply accepted what you learned in these moments as normal and built beliefs, values and stories around the trauma they brought and accepted it as factual.

It's possible you may have built your life around someone else's pain, around someone else's inability to emotionally regulate and around someone else's arrested development. You learned how to feel, how to think and how to process emotions from someone who may have been emotionally dysregulated or arrested in emotional development. You may have normalized someone constantly trying to *fix* things after the trauma, attempting to clean up behind themselves, or someone consistently dismissing your feelings. They dismissed your feelings simply because they did not have the capacity to process their own, let alone yours. From that space, you are not able to develop the skills necessary to self-regulate.

Remember that every time you hear words or re-experience things, they bounce off your map and pull forward whatever previous meaning you gave them or whatever response they were originally encoded in. If you were raised in a highly frenetic environment, this is why your immediate response to things may be chaotic and dramatic, as this is an emergency pattern, laced in adrenaline. And if you were raised in a calm, emotionally regulated household, you may have more of a collected, intentional response that is focused on the well-being of everyone present. The idea here is that however your map was encoded that's the level of intensity it operates in today. Most people who come from severe trauma seek out frenetic environments because it soothes their nervous system. Trauma is the only language their map interprets until they learn differently.

PAUSE WITH JODEE: Allow me to pause and again share that this is not about judgment. This is about awareness. If you are looking back and blaming your parents, that does not serve you or them. If you're looking back and shaming yourself for being that parent, that also does not serve you. We are all doing the best we can with the tools we have at any given moment. I wholeheartedly promise you that there are days that I feel like I completely screwed up my oldest daughter. As a teen mom, I, myself, was arrested in development, while trying to mother another human being. She is a resilient human who allowed me to grow with her. Know that whatever is coming up for you is normal. Allow it to come up and out. If it comes up and you reroute it back in, recycling the same pain, who does that serve? Allow that energy to come up and out.

Arrested Emotional Development

If or when trauma comes before you've had the ability to emotionally regulate, that traumatic experience is like someone throwing a dart into your map, forever anchoring that emotion into that time and space, like the anchor on the boat. Regardless of whether or not you have a secure attachment, this deep, anchored experience leaves you in a space where you are arrested in emotional development. Arrested development, or arrested emotional development, as defined by Horace B. English, is holding onto habits and attitudes suitable to an earlier period of life.[51]

When you are emotionally dysregulated, some of your emotions may feel out of sync, may be challenging to process, and it may often feel like there are triggers all around you. It may take you longer to recover and find balance once an emotionally charged event has occurred. When you are arrested in development, you simply lack the capacity to internally process big emotions and often place blame externally—he makes me so mad, that girl is so . . . , stop pushing my buttons, don't talk to me that way. This inability to self-regulate and internally process emotions is common. If you are reading the statements above and feeling challenged in some way, know that this is all normal. It's not that every single emotion is arrested in development, it's simply the ones that were impacted by the trauma. Until they are acknowledged, validated and processed (you may need a second party to do this fully), they will continue to be triggered.

In arrested emotional development, your external body grows and matures, and your traumatized emotions do not. They remain, forever encapsulated, in that moment in time and in the age in which they were arrested until they are acknowledged, validated and released. An example of arrested emotional development (AED) might be when you witness a fifty-year-old person, who is triggered by something, have an emotional response that's equivalent to that of a five-year-old. Their response is caused by a traumatic event that has anchored an emotion down, and every time it is called forward, the same response will emerge. Because that emotion was arrested in their emotional development with no one present to help them process it, it becomes forever anchored down on their map, encapsulated in the age in which it was arrested.

Now, in the present day, when that emotion is triggered, the response you witness or the response you have is the same as when you were five years old. It's not that this person is emotionally immature, it's that the emotion triggered in that moment immediately took them back to the anchored memory that was originally hijacked and arrested, and the TEA starts spilling. Remember triggers take you back to anchors.

The emotional response that you are witnessing or experiencing is the same emotional response you had in the moment the event occurred. Remember that your neurology creates patterns. This is a patterned response. This is your neurology saying, "I remember this. We're not doing this again." Then it unconsciously jumps into action, protecting you and replaying the previously learned pattern.

What fascinates me is that arrested emotional development was a commonly used diagnosis in the 1950s, yet it has since been removed and replaced with a myriad of other diagnoses, including addictions, anxiety, PTSD, phobias, depression, ADD, ADHD and a few more. Essentially meaning that unprocessed developmental trauma, that results in people being arrested in emotional development, and later being emotionally dysregulated, is the leading source of the majority of the diagnoses listed above. HARD STOP.

I share the hard stop allowing you the time and space to process the idea that if you suffer from any of the diagnoses listed above, or have self-discovered while reading this book that you may have some unprocessed trauma that may lead to one of these, these diagnoses are *symptoms*. They are not root causes. All the diagnoses listed above are symptoms of unprocessed, developmental trauma. They do not stand on their own, nor can they exist outside of a root cause. They come as a result of the action that created them. Understanding that action is imperative for reducing or completely eliminating the symptoms they create. Much like how your story feeds your TEA, your childhood and the way that you learned to regulate your emotions is directly related to all the diagnoses listed above. If you need to set the book down and process that one, please take a moment and do so. Then jump right back in, because healing is possible.

Healing is easier than you think, even if you've already tried multiple things. If this chapter has created some self-discovery, know that this is completely normal. Most of us have been traumatized and have utterly normalized the effects that trauma created for us. Some others may have been diagnosed with the labels listed above and were possibly given medication to help the diagnosis. Learning now about emotional development, emotional regulation, arrested development and emotional dysregulation all stemming from unprocessed trauma may feel overwhelming, which is why I intentionally left this content for the back of the book.

I left it for the end of the book so that you had time to read through, familiarize yourself with and learn all the techniques necessary for healing. You have all the tools you need to start the healing journey. I am very aware that you may need more resources, more guidance and more support than I can offer in this book; however, this book provides not only an incredible starting point but also a super holistic route, free from medication.

The Impacts of Trauma

In chapter 3, we discussed that as a child your map was built by the trusted voices in your world. Starting at conception, the biggest influencers in building your map were your parents (or anyone acting in that capacity— aunts, uncles, babysitters, nannies, older siblings), your teachers, your coaches and medical professionals. You wholeheartedly trusted those adults and the guidance they provided. If those adults did not have a secure attachment and you had a traumatic experience, it paralyzed your ability to emotionally expand. You contracted in that space. You froze, your emotional development ceased, and you were arrested in development.

I can't tell you how many family members and medical professionals told me before the age of eighteen that I was either too tall or too big for my age, as if I was in charge of how tall I was getting or how large my frame grew. Not only was it incredibly damaging for my young, emotionally dysregulated mind, it was also paralyzing. It enhanced my already emotionally dysregulated self. It placed a gigantic anchor on my map. I emerged into this world in the 99th percentile, weighing nine pounds, fourteen ounces, tipping every chart. By four or five years of age, those words paralyzed me. What was anchored onto my map was that something was wrong with me, something made me different from everyone else. Today I stand at five feet eleven inches and wear a size eleven shoe. I've always been tall and have always had a large bone structure. That's simply who I am. Today I embrace it. I healed my map and now honor the idea that I am hella tall. I honor the idea that I am a gentle giant. I love every part of me and honor every single piece of my journey, because without it I would not be this version of Jodee. Know where these things lie on your map and create awareness on the story they tell for you.

During trauma you disconnect from yourself because it's too painful. It's too painful to feel the things you don't know how to feel, especially if you have not established a secure connection and have been left on your own to process these big emotions. What amplifies the challenge is that when in trauma, you are not able to hear your intuition; your gut instinct is hidden in the L1 moments. So instead of listening to your gut feelings, you instead create situations of risk, attempting to stay alive. In trauma you are contracted and fueled by L1 energy, stuck, with zero conscious awareness. Fight or flight is in full swing, and you place yourself in harm's way because the adrenaline feels all too familiar.

Learning is not possible from this space. Survival is the only thing you are focused on. Knowing that you cannot learn from this space and your physiology's only concern is staying alive, your body is unable to integrate or find balance in the world around you or even inside itself. This is the perfect breeding ground for sensory processing disorders, learning disabilities, anxiety, PTSD, depression, substance abuse disorders, addictions, unhealthy relationships and so many other self-soothing behaviors. Cortisol and adrenaline become your normal diet.

Trauma Creates Defiance

When people are hurt by the people who hold authority over them, that gets added to their map. And every time authority shows up, there's a resistance. There's a push back. They are defiant. The intention in being defiant isn't about being difficult, it's simply a protective measure in the eyes of an emotionally dysregulated human. Once we can recognize that as residual trauma from a disconnected/dissociated person versus defiance, it's only then that we can grow. Grow them and grow us. You cannot fix trauma with trauma.

De Bellis explains that "early life adversity can disrupt the body's ability to regulate its response to stress. Experiencing trauma during development along with dysregulation of biological stress systems can adversely impact childhood brain development."[52] Expecting kids who have been affected by, or are still living in trauma, to adhere to or to understand structure and rules means we are also expecting them to be emotionally mature enough to understand those concepts. Most individuals who have been traumatized do not have that capacity. It is our responsibility to recognize the difference.

If a child is not embraced by the village,
he will burn it down to feel its warmth.

—AFRICAN PROVERB

Imagine how many times toddlers fall down when they are learning to walk. They first hold the edge of the couch. Then they get brave and try to stand solo, just learning what balance feels like. Once they have mastered that, they reach one foot out and then maybe the other before that first fall. From that point forward, they know they are onto something. So they get up and try again, and again, and again, and again until they master walking. Never in a million years would a parent, grandparent, teacher, pediatrician, guardian, or whoever give up on that child for falling down on the first or second or tenth try. It's a process. It's all new to them. The reasons they keep trying are twofold. There is no story keeping them outside of trying, *and* there are people surrounding them, encouraging them to get up and try again.

Recovering from trauma is the same process. It's a step-by-step, fall down and get up kind of ongoing process. Expecting kids, adults or yourself to get it right the first time is ludicrous. Allow yourself the time and space to heal in the same way you allow a toddler the time and space to learn to walk. Offer protection. Offer encouragement. Keep yourself out of harm's way. Find an open area where you can expand and heal, free from further trauma or triggering events. Honor the process.

Depending upon the level of trauma you experienced, trauma leaves you conditioned to find all the things around you that might hurt you. Over time you normalize this mechanism when you find yourself in the same patterns of trauma, and this normalized response could literally keep you alive. It's your survival mechanism. However, once the threat is gone, you may continue walking around life, collecting, and resonating on all the things that keep that story alive, which also keeps the adrenaline flowing.

Medicating the Map

If trauma causes emotional dysregulation and arrested emotional development, medicating the map does not change it; it simply reduces your ability to feel. I'm going to take a moment and share my thoughts around medication. You are absolutely allowed to disagree; I would just love to share some insight that is not currently being shared. Although medication temporarily addresses the symptoms you are experiencing, know that drugs also sedate the lower levels of consciousness and lower levels of energy. Once they take effect, you no longer feel any of the emotions associated with L1 and L2 energy— shame, blame, powerlessness, anger. Although it may sound amazing to block those feelings, the medications inhibit your ability to feel anabolic emotions as well.

I wholeheartedly understand that there are certain, isolated conditions that require medication, and I am not telling you to stop taking them. Chemical imbalances are completely different from physiological responses to emotionally charged events. Learned behavior patterns often leave us feeling like we are not in control, especially if they are deeply rooted in our childhoods and were learned as survival tactics. Investigate the difference and understand what your medication is doing to your entire body rather than just masking the symptoms and emotions that feel out of control.

Regardless of the situation, you cannot medicate your map.

Understand that the feelings that emanate from old stories, old anchors, old beliefs and old thoughts only stop happening once you release what's holding them in. Once you do that, their TEA stops flowing. Until you Interrupt the Story and allow the anchors to release, you are simply medicating the symptoms. Our Western approach to medicine, at the moment, is managing symptoms versus addressing root causes. I am being as kind as possible as I share this idea. If you have ever wondered why they push back on holistic medicine and are not huge advocates of teaching people how to heal themselves, it may be because they can only make money from you if you stay *sick*. You can heal your life. Knowing what you know now, what other tools could you start utilizing to affect the change you are seeking with medication?

Commonly Overlooked Trauma Responses

Over-functioning	Constantly giving because you struggle to validate your own self-worth
Under-functioning	Constantly taking because you never learned how to self-regulate
Overworking Fierce Independence	Operating from the anchored, trauma response, validating your worth by constantly working/proving your worth rather than allowing others to help and/or taking a break from work
Narcissism	Early AED, self-protection, learned behavior to protect yourself and all the things you have acquired, lack of attachment
Substance abuse	Drugs sedate the lower level of consciousness/lower LOE, blocking out the ability to feel shame, blame, or victim energy, which is why it's so addictive
Dissociating	Mentally escaping when physically escaping is not possible
Addictions	Addiction to anything that allows your nervous system to self soothe, including shopping, eating, smoking, sleeping, gambling, exercising, cleaning, writing, OCD, etc.
Isolation	Creating distance and isolating yourself from the person(s) and/or events that challenge or trigger the anchor
Projecting	Projecting your feelings onto another versus experiencing and vocalizing what you are feeling
Self-soothing	See addictions
ADD/ADHD	Inability to focus due to living in a contracted state of fight or flight, not knowing who to trust and/or how to self-regulate
Anxiety	Inability to self-regulate, reliving old thoughts that keep the TEA loop engaged
PTSD	Inability to interrupt the memory, story and/or release the anchored memory and emotions, reliving the event over and over again
Processing disorders	Fight or flight is constant, emotionally dysregulated, unable to emotionally regulate long enough to integrate systems

Healing from Trauma

Healing the wound from the initial trauma is how you heal your map. Treating symptoms and hoping to get better is the same thing as collecting leaves hoping the tree stops growing. Most therapy talks *to* the symptom (not the root challenge) and does not address that the symptom was not consciously created (it speaks to the leaves, not the tree or the roots). Emotional roots reside in the nervous system. When trauma patterns are triggered in the body, the body freezes and contracts. When the body feels safe, it releases and expands. People heal once the roots are acknowledged and validated. The power of acknowledging and validating unlocks the nervous system, allowing the anchor to release.

Behavior is a result of the TEA process and an impending storyline. You don't have to keep living the trauma, over and over again. You can take layers one step at a time, one trigger, one TEA loop, one story at a time, and start rewriting your story. Learn to make better pictures. Imagine better outcomes. Future pace yourself living the life you want and then allow the TEA to flow from that point.

> *Treating symptoms and hoping to get better is the same thing as collecting leaves hoping the tree stops growing.*

Traumatized People Cannot Help Traumatized People

If the oxygen you're breathing is from other people's trauma, you're not helping yourself or them. It's challenging to be a resource for someone else when you're still feeling so broken, especially when the broken parts of you are highly uncon-scious. You cannot "survival mode" yourself into healing. You actually have to acknowledge the anchor, validate the energy it brings you and then intentionally release it. Give yourself permission and space to heal.

I'm not sure where I originally heard this, yet it stuck with me. Inside one of my million conversations around trauma, I heard someone use this concept. Ask yourself: How respon-sible am I willing to be for processing what happened to me? Not blameful or shameful, simply responsible.

1. Draw a circle. Then put a line through it, creating two sides to the circle.

2. Ask yourself: Am I willing to be 50 percent responsible for processing what happened to me? If so, I can then control 50 percent of how I move forward from here.

If I am 0 percent responsible, I can then control 0 percent of my next move. When I decide to be 100 percent responsible for myself, I will have the opportunity to 100 percent heal and move forward.

—AUTHOR UNKNOWN

Creating Self-Awareness

Self-awareness is the ability to be so emotionally regulated that you get to choose the emotions you experience versus experiencing them unexpectedly and in a triggered fashion, never knowing what's going to come out. Train the muscle of your brain to respond in alignment. Once a secure attachment has been established and self-regulation is present, your ability to become self-aware amplifies. From this point, the wound heals, the layers improve, your LOE rises, and you no longer seek out the things that fill the void of the nonattachment. From that point, you stop masking. You stop decorating your external world. You start listening at a deep level. You start creating deep, intentional connections. And you start to intentionally turn away from the lower LOEs and start seeking out higher ones. Until the wound heals, none of these things are possible.

You are worthy of healing.

Emotional Regulation, Trauma and Arrested Development Takeaways

- ➢ Feelings are not identities. If you are feeling anxious, you are simply feeling that feeling. You are not anxiety; you are simply feeling anxious.

- ➢ Every time you repeat or retell the story that involves trauma or shifts your energy lower, you're really inviting that energy to re-enter your world. If it's something you're wanting to move past, stop telling the story. Release the energy. It shifts your energy.

- ➢ Healing is a mind and body connection. Create time and space for both to heal.

- ➢ It's not all about emotional regulation, it's about emotional awareness.

- ➢ "In grief we experience sadness. In trauma we experience terror."
  —Starr Commonwealth. You can have grief layered on top of trauma.

- ➢ Childhood trauma is a pre-existing condition that you bring to every relationship.

Questions for Insight

- ➢ What if we allowed our past to be the vehicle that brought us into the best parts of us?

  — The pain taught us how to feel.

  — The grief taught us how to love.

  — The anger taught us that we're worth fighting for.

  — And the stories are actually part of who we were, not who we currently are.

➤ What am I not seeing, or what am I allowing myself to ignore that keeps me in this pattern?

_____

_____

_____

_____

➤ How conscious am I of my ability to self-regulate?

_____

_____

_____

_____

➤ How would I know if I was unable to self-regulate?

_____

_____

_____

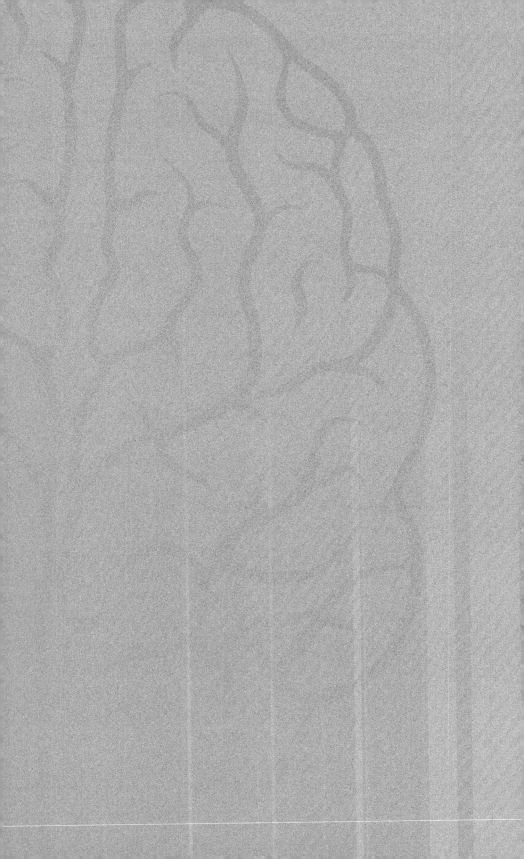

PART III

Healing Your Map

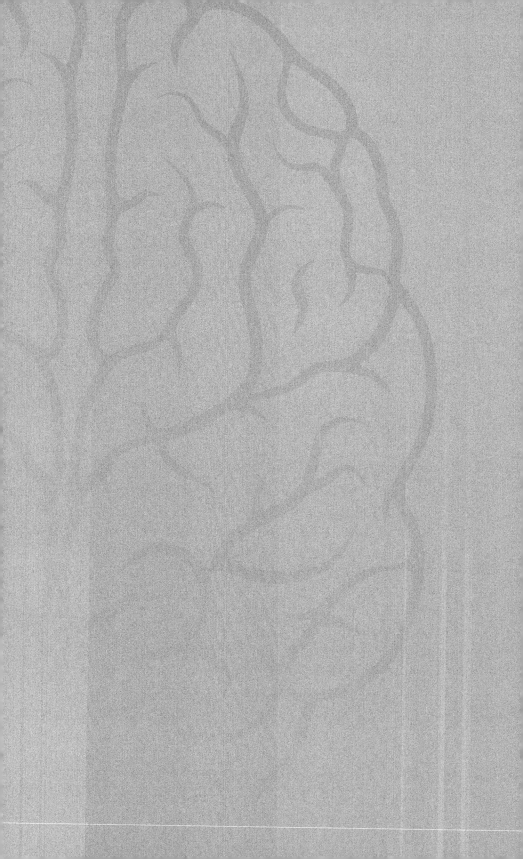

Chapter 14

Healing Is a Verb

*Healing is the intentional energy you
create in an attempt to find wholeness,
joy and self-transformation.*

According to the *Oxford English Dictionary*, healing is the
process of making or becoming sound or healthy again,
tending to, therapeutic. From my perspective, healing is
something you do with great intention. It's an action that you
take. It's a way of life. It's the pause you allow yourself before
taking action. It's the intentional awareness that holds you
outside of drama and further trauma. Healing is the intentional energy you create in an attempt to find wholeness, joy and
self-transformation. It's the subtle yet powerful shift you or-
chestrate that results in transformation, realization and wholeness. Healing from the inside out. Healing the map. Healing
with intention.

Dr. Wayne Dyer said it best, "You attract into your life what
you feel inside. . . . Light eradicates darkness, love dissolves
hate . . . and self-respect attracts the higher energy fields. . . .

What you think of yourself is what you attract from the world." This furthers the idea that your default LOE is what you invite back into your world. The energy that you are sharing with the world, intentionally or unintentionally, becomes the reality you create. Healing your energy and healing your map are both crucial steps in self-regulating and becoming the most whole version of you, essentially living your intentional life.

That self-regulation and wholeness allows you to begin setting boundaries and to begin honoring different layers and areas of your life—your goals, your relationships, your self-care.

If you're not honoring your self-care, how do you get that ideal outcome? If you're not honoring your finances, how do you save money? If you're not honoring your schedule, how do you ever have time? If you're not honoring your healing journey, how do you raise your LOE? Honoring yourself starts with intention.

Once you decide that you are ready to heal, take a moment and recognize that you are out of perceived threat, no longer in danger and no longer living in survival mode. Creating awareness on all three of those may take some time to set in. Keep creating intentional awareness as the old story and juxtaposed layers may be triggered without warning. Take an intentional moment and tell yourself that you are allowed to heal, inviting a new, deliberate reality. Although that may sound easy, this next chapter is full of practical steps you can implement that will bring you closer to yourself transformation. This closing chapter will teach you how to:

- ➢ set your intention,
- ➢ check your energy,
- ➢ trust the process and
- ➢ release the story.

Stay conscious that you've grown into and normalized living in a society that seeks immediate gratification. In the moment you feel hungry, odds are high you may choose to eat on the go, ingesting unhealthy options because they are fast. If you are tired, you may drink energy-consuming coffee, energy drinks and soda. If you are frustrated, you may soothe yourself with drugs, alcohol or nicotine. Rarely do you stop and make healthy, homemade, nutritious whole food. Rarely do you take time for yourself and learn healthy soothing techniques. Rarely do you listen to your body, honoring it, allowing it the time and space to heal. Instead, you ignore the cues it's giving you because you are so focused on getting to the end, accomplishing the goal.

Don't think that there's going to be gold at the end of the road. Instead, value the process and you'll see that the road has been paved with gold all along.

—RUSSELL SIMMONS

One of my favorite quotes was spoken by Russell Simmons. He said, "Don't think that there's going to be gold at the end of the road. Instead, value the process and you'll see that the road has been paved with gold all along." What a passionate explanation that it's not always about what you are going to receive once you accomplish your goal but rather who you become from that journey. If you don't feel like your road is currently paved with gold, slow down and allow yourself time to find it. The gold is there.

Embrace the road. Learn to use your personal power and all the things you are learning along the way to becoming the next version of you. Use that power for what you desire rather than being forced to do otherwise because of physical, emotional or health challenges. That path leads you directly into a better outcome. Would you like to learn how to honor your body, your mind and your spirit, or wait for it to stop working before you take action?

Power serves others, while force is self-serving.

—DR. DAVID HAWKINS

Take a Moment and Simply Breathe

I invite you to find a quiet space and just sit for a moment. Take a deep breath. Silence your phone. Step away from your day-to-day, even if it's only momentarily. Create a place of solace where you can pause for a moment, sit down and breathe. Allow your energy to settle and your mind to quiet. Allow it to get so quiet that you become curious about the world around you.

SMEEPS

Take a moment and reflect on all six of the areas listed below. These are often referred to as your SMEEPS (social, mental, emotional, environmental, physical and spiritual.

Although there are six different areas where you place your energy, I often start with environment because I believe it's the main contributor and the most often overlooked part of your day, but it contributes the most. Understanding how each of the areas below play a role in your life determines your ability to find intentional balance and intentional healing. Taking the time to pause and flow through these six spaces is how you find your center. Learn the healthy vices that balance you.

Environment: Take an intentional moment and observe the temperature. Internalize how it feels on your skin. Is it warm, cold, cool, chilly, damp, humid or maybe dry? Allow your body a moment to simply acknowledge the climate. Next, take a moment and understand the outside weather. Is there a breeze? Is it cloudy, sunny, raining, snowing, or maybe it's simply still. Observe the white noise. What is it that you hear in the background? Is there a freeway that you can hear off in the distance, passing traffic, a train, overhead air traffic, birds, animals, water flowing, leaves rustling, dogs barking? Isolate each sound and take it all in. What are all the textiles around you? Are you inside with carpet, wood floors, fabric or leather furniture, curtains, painted plaster, blankets, pillows, toys? Or are you outside in nature with trees, birds, wildlife? Or maybe in a big city with cars, people, traffic, bustling energy? Or maybe tucked away in your own neighborhood with minimal traffic, kids playing, people walking dogs? What LOE does your environment bring you? What's one thing you could add in that increases that LOE? Where does it fit in your schedule or calendar?

Social: Take a moment and build some inventory around how you spend your social time. Do you spend it with friends? Do you spend it in nature? Do you spend it with family or at work? If somebody gave you an extra day off this week, how would you spend that time socially? Who would you engage with? What are the restaurants, stores and places you frequent? Who are the people you spend the most time with and how do they affect your energy? Who are the people you want to spend the most time with? What is it about their energy that's so inviting? What is the default LOE your social life brings you? The social world around you can tell you a lot about yourself. What's one thing you could add that increases that LOE? Where does it fit in your schedule or calendar?

Mental: What do you think about when you're in these places? Are you taking a moment to take it all in, or are you rushing in and out? How often do you allow yourself to mentally check out? What is the heaviest story you are carrying around? What's the best story you tell yourself that brings you the most energy? How aware are you of your mental capacity and threshold? How do you know when you have exceeded your limits? What actions do you take that stimulate you mentally? What actions do you take when you are mentally exhausted? What is the default LOE of your mental space? What's one thing you could add in that increases that LOE? Where does it fit in your schedule or calendar?

Emotional: Where do you go to find your emotional refuel? How do you fill your own cup? How much time do you spend feeding your emotional brain? What does self-regulation look like to you? How do you know when you're running on reserves? How do you know when you're completely depleted? How would you refill that empty space? How do you know when you are overflowing with expanded, anabolic energy? What draws you into each respective space? What is the default LOE of your emotional life? What's one thing you could add in that increases that LOE? Where does it fit in your schedule or calendar?

Physical: How much physical touch are you allowing in? If someone unexpectedly hugged you, would you embrace them or tense up? How much physical exercise are you allowing your body to experience? Is it the right fit for your body? Do you need physical exertion (running) or physical downtime (slow flow yoga)? How would you know if you were taking great care of your physical body? What is your response when your body speaks to you? Do you honor that message? What is the default LOE of your physical life? What's one thing you could add in that increases that LOE? Where does it fit in your schedule or calendar?

Spiritual: What are the things that feed your soul? Is it praying with a formalized institution? Is it spending time doing any of the things listed above? Is it painting, drawing, writing, speaking, volunteering, serving, teaching, gardening, walking, cleaning, organizing? There are many different ways to feed your spirit. How often are you allowing yourself the time and space to engage in these activities? What is the default LOE in your spiritual life? What's one thing you could add in that increases that LOE? Where does it fit in your schedule or calendar?

Reflecting on all the information you just gathered, what is the overall cadence that it creates for you? If that cadence had a default LOE, what level would it truly represent? Take a moment and understand how that LOE shows up on your map and what territory and energy it invites back to you. Find the highs and the lows of each space. Identify what makes you expand and what makes you contract. Understand the stories behind each space. Then create some conscious awareness around these spaces and become mindful of when they occur, the patterns they bring and the outcomes that occur from these spaces. Learn to slow down and be still. Get present in the spaces. From that space you will have more awareness than ever before and be able to effectively create sustainable change.

Set Your Intention

First things first. Pumpkin seeds don't grow tulips. One thing you have learned for sure in this book is that resonating in a lower LOE does not bring higher LOE results. Contracted energy brings contracted results and vice versa. Setting your intention means creating an intended outcome and then reverse engineering it to find your step-by-step instructions. Reverse engineer your TEA. If there is a behavior, an outcome or an action you would like to take, what layer would you need to heal in order to create that story? What story leads to the thoughts you are looking for? What thought creates that emotion? Taking it a step further, what story do you need to embrace that allows those thoughts to flow? Take time and map it out.

I promise you I did not land where I am by default. It was a mapped out, highly intentional, step-by-step, day-by-day actionable plan. And although that may seem overwhelming, you're going to be here every day anyway. How amazing would it be to wake up every morning and know that you are one tiny step closer to your desired outcome instead of still feeling stuck? Taking action is a decision. Not taking action is also a decision. The question becomes which one will you choose.

Trust me when I tell you that anything is possible. Not only did my journey from wildly uneducated teen mom to finishing graduate school with honors not happen overnight, I guarantee you that my seventeen-year-old self would have *never* been able to comprehend, let alone dream big enough to build the today version of Jodee. It all came as a step-by-step, moment-by-moment, year-by-year journey. It was one class at a time. One powerful story at a time. As I learned more, I knew more. As I knew more, I did better. I consciously chose to engage my highly intentional, highly anabolic, determined Jodee energy. Slowly, over time, I released my contracted self and began to expand. The more I expanded, the more access I had to me, and the loop kept cycling.

When you are contracted, the only solutions you can see are ones that fit inside your contracted world. Whatever you are dreaming up or thinking of is yours for the taking. Just make a plan and map it out. Trust me on this one, I understand there may be parameters that you believe keep you outside of achieving your goal. Whether you have a goal of being the next Academy Award winning Hollywood superstar or the next NFL linebacker, immerse yourself in the world that surrounds that life.

If your dream is to be an NFL lineman and you are a woman who stands five feet two inches, your dream may feel out of touch. Or if your dream is to be the next upcoming Hollywood icon yet you are pushing fifty years old, you can still find yourself in those worlds and expand your energy around your dream. Be intentional and immerse yourself in the life that comes with that dream. Come at it from a different angle and embrace all the different spaces that will raise your LOE inside that same world. Even if you feel like you may never make it on the team, every NFL team has a sports medic, a coach, a trainer, a teacher, an owner and millions of fans. How do you find yourself in one of those spaces versus being directly on the field?

The same thing goes for film or music. Every artist has a producer, a director, a manager, a tour guide, a trainer, a handful of dancers, a band, a makeup artist, a stylist and a myriad of other people that stand right with them. If you cannot get right on top of your goal, immerse yourself in all the other options that create more alignment with who you're trying to be. Much like Russell Simmons shared a few pages back, it's not about the end goal, it's about who you become along the way. Stay present. Take it all in. Allow yourself to expand now, even if it's in the little moments. You may stumble upon something and surprise yourself.

You will never stub your toe standing still.

—CHARLES KETTERING

I invite you to start small and surprise yourself. Make a plan for today that includes the one thing you have been wanting to do—make homemade dinner, work out, read a book, journal, call a friend, meditate, go for a walk, research the thing you want, have the conversation. Then make a one-week plan. Then try a one-month plan. Start slow. Move with intention. It all starts with a thought and a decision. You are worthy of all of it, the new story, the thought, the decision and the outcome it brings.

*Stay curious. Being curious means, you
are not attached to the outcome.*

> **PAUSE WITH JODEE:** You can only work on and affect change
> for the things that are on your map. Creating and dreaming
> for other people is not how this works. You can only change
> your map. Self-care is your only job.

Check Your Energy

Looking back on all six areas shared above, create awareness
around what LOE each of these is contributing to your overall
energy. Self-care includes understanding your energy as well
as understanding what shifts and affects it. Learn to create
boundaries around your energy. Who are you sharing it with?
What is the effect that certain people, places, or things have
on your energy? Are you able to maintain your higher LOEs
when you are in certain crowds, or are you unconsciously
dropping into their default LOE? Create awareness around
how your thoughts shift in these different spaces, creating
unhealthy TEA. Embrace the idea that

> ➢ If I don't say no . . . who will?
> ➢ If I don't set the boundary . . . who's going to set
>   it for me?
> ➢ If I set the LOE, where will the default be?
> ➢ How do I intentionally create that boundary?

Remember it all starts with the story, then the thought.

Create awareness around how you respond to the world around you. Eliminating the trauma response is the goal. Finding self-regulation and an expanded LOE in each of your SMEEPS is where your balance lies. Understanding the role that your SMEEPS play in your healing journey is powerful. Invite vulnerability. Be flexible. Allow time and space to try different things. If you try something and it does not work, that's amazing. You are one step closer to finding what does work.

Understand your circadian rhythm for sleeping and waking. Part of your circadian rhythm is your body's internal time-clock. It wakes you in the morning and puts you to sleep at night. Your body is always speaking to you in very organic ways, yet you may not be listening. Listening to the subtle cues it's giving you helps you fall soundly asleep at night and wake in the morning, having restfully slept. Oftentimes people ignore their circadian rhythm and end up becoming night owls because of their body's response. In a normal circadian rhythm, your body receives cues that it's time to go to bed; however, you may often dismiss them as you are not ready for bed. Due to your continued dismissal of all of its cues, your body believes you are in danger, and it therefore keeps you awake until it perceives the danger has passed. This leaves you wide awake well into the night. Learning to listen to your own body's rhythm, although it may feel way too early some nights, allows you to find your own internal, and very dependable, timeclock. I have not used an alarm clock in nearly a decade, and my body has never felt more rested and balanced.

Before we move into the next section, allow me to share this idea with you. Take a moment and reflect on your done list. Not your to do list or your bucket list, but your *done* list. Pause and take a moment to turn around and look behind you. Take your time as you look back on all the things you have already done. The things you have already accomplished. Look through your SMEEPS at who you were a year ago, five years ago, a decade ago. Look how much you have grown. Look at what you have accomplished. Also know that it's not always about material things. If you are looking back searching for material things and cannot identify them, look at how you've grown into the human you are now. That's worth way more than all the external things people decorate themselves with.

If you've walked a hard road to get to today, please stand up and go look in the mirror. Thank yourself for sticking through it and doing the work. Truly look yourself in the eye and say, "Thank you." Acknowledge and validate that human in the mirror. Thank yourself for still being here. And allow me to thank you for picking this book up and reading all the way into this chapter. That takes huge commitment. Take some time and resonate in the journey that you've walked and the human that it has created. Maybe the material things are still to come. Oftentimes we spend so much time looking at all the things we have yet to do or at all the bucket list things we want to do—the five-year goals, the ten-year goals. Take some time to look back at who you have become. Honor the human that walked that journey. If you feel like you haven't accomplished much, honor yourself for picking up this book. It's all a journey, my friend.

Do all you can with all you have. . . until it brings you more. More wisdom. More joy. More love. More energy. And more joy.

We are convicts of our own beliefs.

—OWEN FITZPATRICK

Trust the Process

We were not put on this planet to be sacrificed for someone else's happiness. We were put here to thrive. We were put here to heal. We were put here to live, to be role models, to be happy. Trust the process. If you are allowing yourself to believe anything different, it's time to write a new story.

Release the Story

Honor who you used to be and allow that person to leave, exit stage left. Think about how old that story is. If that old story of yours is forty years old, would you trust that old version of you to create your new path or to write your new story today? Take a moment, close your eyes, pull up that old energy and thank that version of yourself for keeping you safe and protected all this time. Simply tell that old version of you, "I've got it from here. Thank you for protecting me, but I've got it from here." The greatest game you're playing is the consistent understanding of how your worlds are intertwined—the new you and the old you learning where trauma lies dormant until it's triggered. The more places you can find where that old story lies, the better.

As you start releasing the story, take note of all the places the story has embedded itself. Knowing that your map dominates your world, allow yourself the time and space to learn all the places this old story has woven itself into. What year was the story created? How many other stories are connected to that one foundational story? What emotion did that story provoke, and where do you feel that emotion now in your body? Does it expand, or does it contract? If it contracts you, it's still dominant. It's also quite possible the moment you think it was created was actually the first time it was triggered, which means if the trigger was there, it had to have occurred once already. Allow yourself the time and space to find it. You by no means have to relive it; you simply have to identify where it lives on your map, so you can pull the root rather than trim the weed that grows from it. Once you find the source, create some conscious awareness around it. Is it working towards your goal or against your goal? Does it limit you in any way? The more conscious awareness you have around the limiting belief it has built, the more you understand its root.

Reverse Engineered TEA

Intentional consciousness™

Action/ Ideal Outcome	Emotion	Thought	Story	Potential Triggers	Intentional Anchors
Be more organized	What emotion will being organized create for you?	What thought moves you into action?	What will you be able to do once you are organized?	What might trigger you?	What could anchor this?

Educating Yourself—Future-Proof Your Brain

What happens in your world when you replace the word achieve with allow? Instead of saying *I haven't achieved X yet*, replace it with *I haven't allowed myself to X yet*. Understanding that the power is always yours creates more conscious awareness around what you are allowing.

Identify your triggers and know what engages them. If someone speaks about something you desire while you are present, do you become defensive? Do you create a story around why you have not accomplished that yet? Or are you transparent in saying, *I haven't allowed myself the time or space to work on that yet*. Although that statement may sound crazy to you, once you start living with that level of transparency, two things happen. First, you start getting really clear on your time and your focus. Second, you start attracting other people that are transparent and vulnerable. The best part about this is, knowing that energy self-levels, you start attracting and building a community with really cool, vulnerable humans who are full of clarity and transparency.

The opposite is very true too. When you choose the opposite and live in the excuse-making, closed-off, story-telling scene, it's simply full of exactly that kind of like energy. When you embarrass someone, humiliate them, or shut them down, that's about you and your energy, and it's incredibly damaging for both people involved. Create awareness around which community you are building and who you want to attract. Know which words hold which energy for you. It's not always about healing it but rather simply understanding who you are being and what you are attracting to you. From that space, you are inviting conscious healing.

One of the most powerful words I often play with is the word *yet*. When you beat yourself up and find yourself in a space where you feel like nothing is working, add the word *yet* and watch your physiology immediately follow. It shifts from stuck into having a bit of movement. If you say to yourself *nothing is working*, you are correct. However, if you say *nothing is working yet,* it means there's an answer that has yet to be uncovered. Play with the word *yet* and add it in all the places that feel stuck. It's interesting how the addition of one small word changes the way your brain thinks.

Know What You Want

Interesting fact: most people can articulate to a *T* what they don't want. Yet when I ask them what they do want, they fumble through, pausing, thinking, reflecting, and it all appears a bit confusing for them. Oftentimes they shift into wanting all these material things. Take a moment to think it through.

If you could feel any way you wanted to feel,

If you could be anything you wanted to be,

If you could manifest any emotion possible,

What would it be?

What *do* you want?

Once you put your finger on a few things, start journaling around them. How do you draw more of that energy into your life? When you start spending more time resonating in what you do want, resonating in the solution, you start telling the Universe (or whatever deity you pray to) more of this please! You start attracting the solution to you and more energy that matches the solution rather than attracting more of the challenge. Start telling people what you want. Write it down every day. Change your screensaver on your phone to remind you of your goals. Set a timer on your phone that goes off every day at a certain time reminding you of what you're working towards and who you're becoming. I have been practicing this for the past ten years, as of today, my current daily reminders are:

My only job is to create awareness.

My capacity to give and receive expands infinitely with the Universe.

Prosperity is my birthright.

Every single day these pop up individually on my phone at different times, constantly reminding me of who I am becoming. Stay conscious of the story and the thoughts your TEA needs to make your dream a reality. As you put all these things into place, you will start shifting your energy towards what you want versus what you don't have. The catabolic energy will dissipate. The contraction will release. You will begin to expand and step into that version of you that you've always dreamed of.

Understand Your Shadow

This is crucial information. This next piece of information was mentioned briefly in chapter 9, yet it's incredibly fundamental to your success. It's also the part that most people miss. As you step into the new version of you, the old version of you will still be alive and well in what we refer to as *your shadow*. Not to get all philosophical on you, but know this, your shadow can run interference like no other. As you start growing into this new version of you, there is still this old version that remembers who you used to be. It remembers how you felt.

It remembers the struggle. It remembers how challenging it was with every part of its being. It is embedded into your map, and it so badly wants to save all the other people that are still in that old energy. No one saved you. You made the decision to take the next step. That's exactly the same journey that everyone else has to make. Remember that you are only in charge of your map, and you can only change your map. Saving other people is not a thing.

Your shadow is so fluent in your old story and in those old, contracted LOEs that it can very easily be influenced and taken off track. It's so used to being contracted that you won't even notice it until it's too late. You will not notice that you have dived off the deep end trying to help a friend until you find yourself deep in the water, alone. You have to shut down the old energy. You have to stay conscious of your shadow. If you are not conscious, you may get two steps ahead and then take twelve steps back because you start soaring ahead and then something triggers you. Something from your past engages your energy, someone calls you, someone makes a comment about your journey, and the next thing you know you find yourself trying to save all your friends and family. Or you find yourself in the middle of someone else's drama, and you try to *fix* it for them with your new skills. Remember:

No one is broken.

You are only in charge of you.

That is your shadow.

That is your old story.

The longer you stay in that old energy, the longer it will keep you there. There is no possible way to be in two places at once. There is no way to split your energy. There is no way to be contracted and expanded at the same time. There is no way to be anabolic and catabolic at the same time. You are either with your old shadow or you are the new version of you. It's very common for people to be very confused here. You can absolutely help people from your new default, expanded energy. You can help people from your new position. You can help people from your new story. You can help people with your new boundaries in place. You are the one who has to stay grounded. You can build boundaries around how you are willing to help and how you are not willing to help. You may say things like *I'm more than happy to help* and *insert your boundary here.*

If people are not honoring your boundaries, they are not for you. Step away from the people who do not honor your boundaries. I know this is hard to hear and the push back is real. You are worth healing. Your journey is worth continuing. Honor yourself and your boundaries. Step away from the people who are afraid to be great. Stand up. Stand out. Step into it. The simplicity of human behavior is something we far too often overlook. We complicate things. We make things harder than they really are. Human behavior is incredibly complex yet very simple. Put time and space between anyone or anything that hinders your ability to heal and expand.

Decide that it's you.

Decide that you are in charge of what happens.

Decide that it's you that gets to choose how you feel.

Decide that it's you that gets to make the decision.

Decide that it's you that gets to accomplish your goals.

Things only change once you decide that it's you that matters first. Take ownership of your own feelings. Those come from within.

You are enough.

You are ready now.

Honor your voice.

Believe in your value.

Set your intention.

Honor your story.

Trust the process.

Create a Space

A year or so ago I started writing all of this content around intentional consciousness because I truly didn't believe that people spent enough time focusing on what they want and on how they want to build it. Start creating intentional spaces and building intentional anchors. Be creative with this next section because your options are endless.

The next time you go on vacation or visit your favorite spot, even if it's only to your favorite yoga class, bring a scented candle or some essential oils with you (be responsible with both) and anchor that scent with that activity. Allow the scent to fill all your senses with that intense memory, taking it all in. Then bring that candle or oil home and keep it on hand for each time you want to revisit that moment. When you light the candle or use the oil, the smell will immediately take you back. You can place the essential oils on all kinds of things in your car, in your bedroom, in your home, in your office, forever introducing that calm, familiar, expanded feeling into whatever you do. Set an intentional anchor.

This same thing can be duplicated for anything you want to anchor. Again, be intentionally creative. Anchors can be placed anywhere for anything. Turn your expanded energy into purpose. This creates a natural release for emotions. Remember, awareness equals access. The more awareness you have around what you want, the more access you will have to the road that brings it. You can build anchors into meditation, journaling, silence, movement, reading, exercising, cooking, building community or just about anything you can imagine. Also know that rebuilding and reworking your map takes time. When you start something new, odds are high you aren't quite fluent in it. It feels quirky. You may want to throw the towel in, yet what keeps you moving and working through the rough patches is the LOE that is driving you. Stay conscious of your energy always.

Hardwood grows slowly.

— JEWEL

Reflections

How much different would your world be if:

- ➤ You stay conscious of the role all your SMEEPS play and the LOE they bring.

- ➤ You embrace the idea that energy is always present. It's simply about being conscious of what expands you and what contracts you.

- ➤ You focus more energy on what you do want and practice the energy that brings it, resonating on the idea that you are a work in progress.

- ➤ You focus on creating intentional anchors, big *T* truths and writing new stories.

- ➤ You start creating transparent, vulnerable conversations around what you want.

- ➤ You become conscious of what you are hearing when people talk. What are you drawn into? What do you repel from?

- ➤ You always remember that pumpkin seeds don't grow tulips. You are responsible for your own energy and the outcomes it creates around you.

- ➤ Instead of believing that you're struggling, you view it as a transitional phase. The moon isn't always visible from where you're standing, yet that doesn't mean it's not there.

The only way to interrupt generational trauma is to repair your current map.

Become You

Learning to make better pictures, imagining better outcomes, and future-pacing yourself living the life you want is how change begins. You do not have to have the whole thing planned out, you just have to have to commit to the process.

Create a picture of your ideal self.

What are you wearing?

Where is the location?

How do you feel inside?

What does it smell like?

What is the default LOE of that future version of you?

Now take that picture and slide it next to the current version of you.

Flip the current version of you over so it's face down.

Leave it face down.

Resonate on your new picture.

Make it bigger.

Amp up the color.

Lay your favorite soundtrack over it so it plays each time you see it.

Amp up the smell.

Create the feeling.

Amp it up just a bit more.

Add in all the cool details.

Take notes.

Memorize this picture.

This is you.

Build the story that goes with this version of you.

Jot down the thoughts that align with the future you.

Repeat this process as often as necessary.

How much more love can you take in? How much more happiness can you find? How much more success can you allow yourself to experience? How much more money can you make? How much more of the world can you see? How much more of yourself can you experience if you simply stop and intentionally and consciously allow it? Once you realize that the experiences you are having are directly connected to what you are allowing, it's only then that things will begin to change. You are the author of your story. The pen is in your hand. The only thing standing between you and your goals is your permission.

Chapter 15

Stories That Expand You

Honestly, I'm honored every time a new coaching client hires me. I am honored that they trust me with the most intimate details of their life. I am honored that they allow me to witness their self-discoveries. I am honored to hold space and help them explore their map as they search for their best solution. I often say my only job is to create awareness. That awareness is pulled forward by asking questions. Not just any questions, but instead highly intentional, thought-provoking questions that result in my clients doing a powerful, trans-derivational search, investigating every crack and crevice of their map for the answers. It's those exact searches that pull forward the most content, allowing incredible self-discovery.

I learned very early on that coaching the energy behind the story is way more powerful than coaching the story it-self. Imagine if I coached every story you shared with me. You would essentially need me to help you process every single story you believed was true. My coaching sessions wouldn't be very productive because coaching every little detail, through every story, does not help you move forward. It just keeps you in that energy, in those little *t*, contracted beliefs. I instead coach the energy. My focus is to understand the lens with which you are trying to process what you are experiencing. I get curious about the map you are using to navigate that story, and then coach you through making tiny, little map edits that lead you to different outcomes.

One Tiny Degree

Imagine you decide to sail to Hawaii from Malibu. It's roughly a 2,500-mile journey. Remember that Hawaii is a very small series of islands in the gigantic Pacific Ocean. This journey will take some serious planning and precise navigation. Mapping your route, stocking your boat, and planning for a two-to-three-week journey are all necessary. But know this, if your navigation system was one simple degree off, you would never hit your target. That one degree would completely change your final destination, and you would totally miss Hawaii, possibly leaving you stranded at sea. One tiny degree. That one tiny degree is insurmountable as it adds up mile by mile by mile, compounding its effect. Embrace the idea that most unhealthy anchors create that same compounded effect. It's often the smallest shift or the unassuming anchored belief that keeps you away from achieving your goals. The changes that create the biggest impact are simple one-degree shifts. They are not gigantic, huge, life disrupting events. They are one tiny shift after another.

For this chapter I would love to reflect on some of the tiniest shifts I have made with clients that became the most impactful pivotal spaces of their lives. They all had one tiny anchor, one limiting belief, or one old story that created the largest compounded effect, forever changing the trajectory of their lives. One tiny shift changed everything.

Note: I have changed the names, identities and/or genders to protect my clients.

Quitting Is Not an Option

I had the honor of coaching an up-and-coming leader of a local mortgage company. This rising star, Steve, was twenty-eight years old and already deep into making six figures. He was running a small team and was referred to me for help sorting a few things out. Steve was struggling with his team and had made the decision to quit his job the day we connected. Although he had not formally shared the news with his employer, moments before our session, he had formally written his letter of resignation.

As Steve and I dove in, I listened to his story. Steve revealed that he was running a very young and eager, hardworking team. They were being dramatically overworked as most of them were on-call eighteen hours a day. They were starting to request time off or would not respond to work calls due to the negative impact the overtime was making on them. Because of this, Steve's numbers were starting to decline. Yet he knew that if he didn't protect his team, they would all quit, and his numbers would be even worse. He needed them to stay on board, but the only way they were willing to stay was as if they had a little bit of time off, himself included.

I listened to him articulate. I heard what he was saying. It was apparent to me there was something deeply anchored on Steve's map, preventing him from taking time off and creating the paralyzed response he was experiencing. After asking some clarifying questions, I asked him one of my favorites:

How old were you the first time you remember running this pattern? He was a bit perplexed by the question, as people often are, so I repeated it again, word-for-word. How old were you the first time you remember running this pattern? The silence was deafening.

Silence is my favorite tool in coaching. Silence always does the heavy lifting. It's the sound you experience when someone is searching through their map. Silence is the most powerful indicator that a coach has done their job. One thing you can always count on me for is holding that exact space—space of pure and utter silence. When my clients fall to silence, so do I. I stay absolutely silent until they speak next, regardless of how long it takes. Seconds turn into a minute, and those minutes start to pile up. The silence remains. I stay silent because I know that's where the heavy lifting is done. Silence is what coaching is all about. Effective coaches ask powerful questions and then zip it. Filling that once uncomfortable space with my voice only furthers my clients' pain. Allowing the silence allows my clients the guided time and space necessary to search through their map until they find the answer they are searching for.

"I was eleven," he responded four full minutes later. "I was eleven years old and I had just quit little league." Steve went on to tell me the story about losing a game and his dad telling him, "If you're not going to play full out don't bother playing at all." So here he was, seventeen years later, not playing full out and instead choosing to protect the humans he was so deeply invested in; he was ready to walk away from a $250,000 a year income because of an unconscious anchored belief that his dad set nearly two decades prior. It was an anchor so deeply embedded that it was about to change the trajectory of Steve's life forever. We spent the balance of the session removing the anchor and the belief—and deleting the resignation letter. One session, a seventeen-year-old anchor removed and the career of a lifetime salvaged.

Everyone Needs a Coach

Much like the idea that all children need parents, all leaders need coaches. And truthfully, in my humble opinion, everyone needs a coach. Great coaches help you master the way you use your map. Self-mastery is the art of learning to understand the most effective way to consciously use your map. The more you understand about your map and the perspective it builds for you, the more access you have to the reality that perspective builds around you. And the more you understand that although your parents meant well, they may have placed some incredibly unhelpful, outdated anchored beliefs on your map that remain fixed there. Understanding or realizing the negative effects they leave in their wake creates a new level of awareness. It's that exact awareness that allows movement and brings change.

The Voice of Freedom

In a very recent coaching session, I was coaching another company owner through a challenging space. She was living in a state of frustration because every time she tried to use her voice she paused, fearing that people may judge what she said and then decide they didn't like her. Although she was their boss and they answered to her, she feared their responses. Here she was running a multimillion-dollar company yet afraid to freely use her voice.

You can predict my question, right? I leaned in and asked, "How old were you the first time you remember this feeling?"

"Oooooo . . ." she responded, and then the silence arrived.

Her pause was not quite as long as I expected, yet her response surprised her. It was right in alignment with Steve's. She was eleven years old when her family relocated to a new town. This new town included a new school and new friends. As a young, tender preteen, her fear was incredibly real. *What if they don't like what I say? Will they still like me?* repeated over and over as her dominant thought. Leaving her cozy home and all her friends behind meant she had to make new friends in her new town. She was officially the new kid on the block and the new kid at school. Not only that, but her fear was exacerbated upon the arrival of her new baby brother a few months later. Once she realized how much presence that moment still held on her map, nearly fifty years later, she allowed herself to process the original emotion and release it. Fifty whole years. From that space, she began using her voice with authority and confidence. She became vulnerable, brave and nearly invincible. To say that her company is thriving would be a complete understatement.

Frozen in Time

This last example is still one of my favorite clients. Laura was a scientist who normalized burning the midnight oil. She poured herself into her work for nearly two decades, eventually creating a drug that cures a very prominent and often diagnosed chronic disease. She was midway through a multi-year contract with the National Institutes of Health (NIH) and was awaiting their acceptance of the drug when she found herself paralyzed. She had a team of people helping her, her product was performing, and she was in a stable relationship, yet she was completely miserable, stuck and paralyzed inside her own world.

Her relationship with her partner of more than ten years, as she disclosed, was more about security, stability and the luxurious lifestyle it offered than it was about love. It was completely void of intimacy. She very much enjoyed the attention, the gifts and the incredible lifestyle her partner brought to her, yet they had zero chemistry. It was something he simply did not offer her, yet she desperately wanted. She dreamt of coming home from work and enjoying her partner, spending time together, both in and out of the bedroom, yet it never happened. No part of her was willing to leave.

She dreamt of creating a new life where her energy could expand. As she shared her dream, her energy shattered her previously stagnant energy. Her goal was to move to the other side of the country and work outside of her office walls, raising and training horses full-time. Her dream was to train horses for nonverbal kids and spend the balance of her life giving back. Her only challenge was that she had yet to find someone to fund that dream. I shared with her my go-to remedy that works for most of my clients, myself included.

Show them your soul. They'll give you the money.

We dove through the same powerful questions, and the evidence that she pulled forward shocked her. Her parents divorced when she was a young child. No one ever circled back to make sure that she recovered from that contracting, devastating break. From that point forward, Laura sought out things to soothe her contracted spirit, things that represented safety and security. She placed those things high above feeding her soul. Laura came alive as she articulated each and every detail of her equestrian dream. Words cannot describe the energy she exuded. She was widely expanded and even more excited about all the lives her dream would touch. She had the entire thing planned out; and by the end of our twelve sessions, she had even found a way to fund her beautiful dream. The new lifestyle would definitely not be as glamorous as the life she was currently living, yet it utterly and completely fed her soul. Needless to say, she still works at NIH. Contracted. Safe. Feeding her L1 energy. Not everyone is ready for change.

Childhood Legacies

Your childhood anchors only leave once you evict them. Although powerful leaders often unknowingly use their childhood legacies as leverage for effective leadership, they also often lead very unhealthy, unfulfilled lives. As noted earlier in the book, overworking is a trauma response. Working hard and then taking time to recharge is the key in finding balance. Most overachievers struggle with that concept. Your childhood is deeply embedded into your map. The more conscious awareness you have around it, the more personal power you gain back. The less you have, the more it controls you.

Some of the most influential leaders in the world are the ones with the most challenging childhoods. It's the same resilience that carried them through that's fueling them today. It's the stories of survival that create the resilient leaders who refuse to give up, the relentless, against-all-odds survivors. Know that it is completely necessary to stop and feed your soul. Find the things that make you grin. Find the things that awaken your creativity and expand your being. It's those exact things that raise your LOE, automatically raising your waterline. That's how you draw more and more success into your life. Work hard and then play harder.

What Makes a Good Coach

Being a good coach means having the ability to listen to the energy behind the words. Behind the patterns. Behind the stories. It's about having the ability to listen to what people are saying rather than listening to the content of what they're saying. It's about understanding the energy that built that pattern. It's understanding the emotional age of the pattern that built that energy. It's about having the ability to listen at such a high level that you can hear what the client isn't saying. And then, with that info, being able to create the most effective, thought-provoking questions to invite powerful self-discovery for the client. That self-discovery allows the energy to shift, releasing it from its contracted state and allowing it to expand. That's what effective coaching truly is.

When you are in survival mode, not only do you have no idea that you are there, yet you also have no idea there are more options than the one you are fixated on. The reason you feel stuck is because you only see one way out, one way to do things, or one solution to your challenge. That one solution is often inaccessible for you, creating the idea that you are stuck. It's only when you shift into a state of awareness and out of that catabolic cloud that you realize there are other options. This is why asking questions works. It takes you into a different part of your brain. It forces you to answer questions from a different space, inviting self-discovery and creating a new perspective. This is precisely why giving advice is so ineffective. It's not that you don't know what to do, it's that you are in the wrong state to be able to take action that someone else is suggesting. Changing your state first and raising your LOE is step one. Releasing the contracted energy allows you to expand. From that space, solutions appear.

Immerse yourself in the process—release yourself from the expectation.

The man on top of the mountain didn't fall there. He pushed himself way outside of his comfort zone. He took a chance and allowed himself to think differently instead of remembering what didn't work last time. He knew that if he wanted his perspective to change, he would need to change the way he viewed things. Instead of looking at the mountain like it was an insurmountable task, he decided to view it as a quest, as a personal challenge. He learned about hiking. He learned about climbing. He changed his story. That new story brought new thoughts. Those new thoughts made it feel possible . . . and he climbed.

When your internal audio matches your external world, you project clarity.

For All the Parents

I cannot leave you without sharing this concept. Allowing kids to find and authenticate their voice and build powerful maps are what sets them apart from the masses. You can either teach kids how to use their voice or you can shush them. Know that most times you are doing both. You teach them to speak up and use their voice; yet when they try to use it with you, you don't like it. The art of this space is teaching kids (and others) how to use their voice appropriately and to be able to speak up and share their energy with you. Not only is it imperative to use it with you at home, it's also incredibly healthy for them to learn to use it with their teachers, their coaches, their doctors and anyone else they may need to speak directly to, without being reprimanded.

When they can learn to advocate for themselves, they have a skill that most adults currently do not have. If they cannot use their voice with you because you think it's disrespectful, how can you expect them to go out in the world and use their voice with everyone else? When kids do not learn how to use their voice appropriately, it hinders their ability to function as a healthy adult. It hinders their ability to advocate for themselves. It makes complete sense that they get out in the world and cannot access their inner authority. They get stuck, paralyzed, and end up in L1 situations because their skills did not match what they bumped into outside their safe walls at home. They simply don't know how to use their voice. Learning how to use their voice appropriately and respectfully and learning to agree to disagree and still be friends starts at home. Learning to advocate for themselves, to stand in their own authority and to maintain a level of respect, both for themselves and for others, puts them lightyears ahead of their peers.

Helping kids learn to use their voice starts small with encouraging them to use the words and speak in complete sentences (to the best of their capacity for their age and development) and then slowly expanding that. Find gentle people in your community who like kids and are helpful in their learning. Have them learn to speak to the local librarian and request their favorite books. Teach them to greet the neighbors on your daily walk, asking the neighbor how they are doing and waiting for their response. Teach them to greet the mailman if you are home and it's possible. Have them talk and engage with the pediatrician, answering questions for themselves (as appropriate). Have them learn to order their food in a restaurant. Even if they don't get it right the first time, acknowledge them, validate them and encourage them to try again.

Shouting at them, embarrassing them, or humiliating them invites more shame, blame, and contracted energy and makes it even more challenging to try again. Help them normalize using their voice and advocating for themselves. If they can learn to use their voice with all the people who have helped them build their map, they will also know how to use their voice in the world. If you are reading this and it resonates for you personally, you can edit this space too. This book is full of tools you can use to go back and edit the pattern. Take the risk. Edit the pattern. Find your voice.

All the success in the world started with a risk. I recently heard someone share this concept about evidence, alluding to the idea that most successful things started with a lack of evidence. Henry Ford had zero evidence that his idea would roll. The Wright Brothers had zero evidence that their idea would take off. Rosa Parks had absolutely zero evidence that her idea would cause people to stand. Sometimes the most profound ideas just need someone brave enough to try them.

Growth Is Messy—Embrace It

Personal growth is messy. Personal growth takes you on a journey of self-discovery. It's the place where you uncover all the things about yourself that you did not want to know, or possibly had no idea were even there or how to deal with them. It's kind of like the first time you learn how to make a cake. You gather all the ingredients, find a big bowl to mix in, pull out the mixer and start baking. The only way you learn that you cannot lift the mixer out of the bowl while it's moving is by doing exactly that. Before you know it, you have spewed chocolate all over your kitchen, your shirt is covered in flour, and there are chocolate chips rolling around all over the floor and cake mix dripping from your ceiling. At this point, you toss the cake in the oven, having no idea what to expect once it comes out. As the timer goes off, you pull out a perfectly imperfect cake. You did it! And even as you look behind you to the pile of dishes and the dirtiest kitchen ever, you revel in the idea that you have expanded. You accomplished your goal. Allow the mess, friend. Get dirty. Your growth will shine through. So the next time you find yourself idolizing someone else's cake, remember the journey it took them to get there. Although you may not see the evidence, know there was a gigantic mess at one point.

Your performance is the gift—not the outcome of your performance.

Vulnerability Creates Alignment

As a coach, I wholeheartedly know that I cannot take a client anywhere I have not been myself. Yet, odds are high that if they showed up in my world, we share some mutual energy that attracted us to each other. Whether that's old childhood energy, past traumas or present-day energy, our ability to attract like energy is ongoing. My energy is beyond diverse as I've experienced a considerable amount of territory. From the hometown I hail from to the world I currently live in and everything in between, I truly can say that I get people. I understand where they are coming from. I know where they have been. From my own personal history to the amazing adventure my older daughter took me on, to having two beautiful kids seventeen years apart, to the journey of being a solo parent for nearly three decades, human behavior is my fluent language. I cannot even begin to fathom where I'd be had I not allowed myself to be vulnerable and experience my life in the way that I did.

Find your center. Identify all the juxtaposed positions you unknowingly place yourself in. If you spend time and money going to school only to take a job that undermines your presence, that creates misalignment for you. If you read self-empowering books in the morning and then watch *Law & Order* to fall asleep at night, understand how those two spaces collide. Your words say one thing, but your energy says another. You have one intention yet saturate your brain with another. You have no idea of the clarity that you are missing out on. What old stories or normalized old LOEs do these latter experiences feed for you? Learn how to remove those anchors. Take intentional action and release the old, contracted, catabolic energy.

I am only fluent in these spaces because I walked those same roads. I used to have these same juxtaposed habits. Then I stopped being a victim to my old story. I stopped being a victim of the stories people told around me. I literally stopped caring what people thought of me. I stopped keeping people comfortable. I quit playing small, and I started being highly intentional. I started taking care of myself first and started living from a different default. I started using my voice even if it made other people uncomfortable.

For my entire life, people have had something to say about me—they were overly concerned with my lifestyle, where I choose to live, who I choose to associate with, how educated I am or am not, why I choose to be a single parent, and why I move so many times. It is all so confusing to them. It's confusing to them because they are using their map while attempting to understand my world. Not realizing that each one of those wild decisions I intentionally made were exactly what created this today version of Jodee. Trust me when I say that I know exactly what I am doing. Had I stayed in the box that made them comfortable, I would have had to remain stuck and contracted, playing very small.

Although I cannot put my finger on it, there was a pivotal moment in my life when I decided to stop playing small. Decades ago I chose to step around the labels that had been placed upon me and leave them with the people who assigned them. I decided to stop caring what people thought and to simply do whatever the hell I wanted. It was at that same moment that I realized I couldn't be in two places at once, and I had to make some serious changes. I started creating alignment with my words, my actions and my lifestyle, allowing my wholeness to emerge. For anyone who knows me, playing small is not an option. We often joke in my family that not only am I not getting in the box, I have no idea that a box even exists. It is not on my radar. My philosophy is play big or go home.

I've always been a dark horse. What an absolute gift that was.

Remember that the girl who is writing this book was once a wildly uneducated teen mom who not only finished graduate school but graduated with honors. If I can accomplish all these things, you absolutely the hell can too. And honestly speaking, did you come this far to only come this far? You have made it this far in life and have made it all the way to the last chapter of this book. You have gained all the knowledge on how to live the life you've always dreamed of. Are you ready to kick the doors open and take what's yours?

Challenge yourself.

Challenge your story.

Challenge your energy.

Get really intentionally clear on what you want.

And then GO GET IT!

As I wrap this chapter up, I'd love to create some awareness around the idea that your life dramatically changes the day you realize every day is a gift. Every challenge is a gift. Every obstacle, every relationship, every hardship, every single opportunity you get to experience is a gift. It's those exact experiences that make you the human you are. When you live in alignment with the idea that everything happens because it's supposed to and there are no mistakes, you start living differently. You start finding freedom in your everyday life, no longer consumed with other people's opinions, previous decisions and all the other details that are completely out of your control. If it's not something you can directly control, allowing it to control your energy is an absolute choice. Choose wisely.

Every challenge is a gift. Every obstacle, every relationship, every hardship, every single opportunity you get to experience is a gift.

Things I Know for Sure

- ➢ Who you are as a person is always editable.

- ➢ Your level of energy absolutely determines the experience you have.

- ➢ What happened to you is not who you are, it's simply a spot on your map.

- ➢ Being humble carries you further. Find appreciation for the people who have challenged you because it's those exact experiences that showed you who you are capable of being.

- ➢ Spend time thinking about what's possible instead of remembering what happened yesterday.

- ➢ The labels people place on you are about them, not you.

- ➢ Allow yourself to be the lotus. Grow through the muck.

- ➢ Take big changes that expand who you are as a human being.

- ➢ Always know there are no mistakes.

- ➢ You are exactly where you should be.

- ➢ Start from where you are and use what you have.

- ➢ Be flexible. Your world expands at the capacity that you do.

- ➢ Your goals are not the destination; they are simply the vehicle to your next step.

➢ Let people see your soul. Operate from a level of energy that allows your soulful vibe to shine through.

➢ You are one choice away from the life you want. Choose with great intention.

Conclusion

Congratulations! You've mastered the content of your map! Take a moment and reflect on all the things you've learned. Chapter by chapter you answered question after question, uncovering a myriad of things that were previously out of touch for you. You found content that answered questions you had yet to ask. You found information, patterns, anchors and feelings that had yet to be explored. You remained vulnerable, allowing things to surface as you sorted through all of it, piece by piece. The collection of all the content together tells the story of your map.

In chapter 1, you gained a basic understanding of the principle of the map and the territory and why your map matters.

In chapter 2, you uncovered how maps are built, what keeps them together, the story you build around them, how you hide behind masks, the power of awareness, the states of consciousness and what it means to have psychological sunburn.

In chapter 3, you uncovered how you normalize your chosen vice, how your collective energy is created, the default LOE it creates and draws in around you, the weight of shame and your childhood mirror. You also discovered how your childhood shows up in the present day, how you communicate and the age of your emotional capacity.

In chapter 4, you learned how to edit your map, about the compound effect, about the functions of a parent, how things get lost in translation, how to feel your feelings, how to dream big and how to create a new map that leads you to present day goals as well as your long-term, big-dream goals.

In chapter 5, you learned the basics of the six layers of human behavior, what they are comprised of, how they work, and why they matter.

In chapter 6, you uncovered your awareness and the multiple layers of your map, including NLP, expanding and contracting, spilling TEA, anchors and triggers, the powerful stories we tell ourselves, trauma and emotional regulation, the idea that awareness equals access and what vices you use to manage your current map.

In chapter 7, you uncovered foundational information about NLP, KAVOG and how you take information in, encode it and store it for later use. You learned about values, the role they play and even how to find your own. You learned about beliefs, the role they play and the power they hold. You learned about your patterns, where they were built and how you have normalized them.

In chapter 8, you uncovered your emotional foundation. You learned where your thoughts emanate from, how emotions are created and what your behaviors are founded in. You discovered your biggest challenges and frustrations; and you identified your triggers, both internal and external, and learned how to access them. You learned about the TEA model and the reverse TEA model. You learned how your emotions are encoded and what decisions you make around them. You learned about TEA loops—how they are built, what keeps them engaged and how to open the loop.

In chapter 9, you explored Intentional Consciousness and the levels of energy (LOE). You learned about anabolic and catabolic energy and how each makes you either expand or contract. You learned about the patterns created by the seven levels of energy, Scissor Syndrome and the conscious middle. You discovered how your LOE plays a role in your everyday life. You learned where your default LOE is, what access that provides for you and the role your childhood story plays in that space.

In chapter 10, you uncovered the concept behind anchors, triggers and buttons. You learned how your anchors and triggers were created and who can remove your buttons. You learned about finding anchors, the meaning you create around them, what they pull forward for you, how they serve you and most importantly, what LOE they are anchored in. Lastly, you learned what KAVOG response your anchors trigger, what TEA they create, what beliefs they build and how to remove them.

In chapter 11, you explored the powerful stories you tell yourself, how stories work, how anxiety (and a myriad of other things) works, how to identify a story and all the different things that live inside your stories. You learned about conscious stories—where their roots are and how to challenge that story. You briefly learned about dissociated healing.

In chapter 12, you uncovered how to Interrupt the Story as well as the foundation of story. You learned about masking the pain and ego versus soul.

In chapter 13, you learned about emotional development, emotional regulation and dysregulation, and the four universal needs. You learned about trauma—the different levels and responses and how the remnants of trauma show up inside your physiology. You learned about arrested emotional development and the impact it creates. You learned about medicating or not medicating your map, how to heal from trauma and how responsible you are willing to be in that process. You learned about self-awareness in these tender spaces and what you can allow your journey to teach you.

In chapter 14, you uncovered how to set your intention, check your energy and trust the process. You learned how to breathe. You learned all the areas where residual trauma and old stagnant, unproductive energy may still reside. You learned how to release the story and how to future-proof your brain. You learned how to understand your shadow and the potential energy it has the power to draw in. You learned how to create the space and simply become the version of yourself that you have always dreamed of being.

And finally in chapter 15, you took a glimpse inside a few stories that brought it all full circle. You found yourself in other people's stories. You understood firsthand how each piece of your life is connected to the next step. You learned about parenting, about coaching and that growth is messy; and I shared with you the things I know for sure.

You have all the tools you need for your next step. This beautiful journey of life is yours for the taking! Remember:

Happiness is not something that happens to you, it's something you get good at by practicing. So is the opposite. Choose wisely.

Acknowledgments

As many of you know, I have led an incredibly colorful life that has allowed me to connect with a myriad of people. Without every moment of my life, the good, the bad, the ups, the downs and everything in between, none of this would be possible. Whether you have walked the path with me or find yourself inside of one of my stories and remember that moment of my life, know that I cherish your presence and the joy it brought. Every one of you is a part of my journey and I appreciate you.

My deepest appreciation goes out to the brilliant humans who knowingly or unknowingly helped make this book possible. With your guidance and support, directly or indirectly, you shared yourself without reservation and helped make this book possible. You listened. You taught. You guided. And you selflessly helped bring my idea to life. I just wanted to take a moment and extend some incredible love and energy to you.

I would love to give a special thanks and honor a handful of people. It was your life's work and selflessly shared wisdom that lit the path of my journey.

My parents (aka Gib & KG)

Dr. Richard Bandler

Dr. Paul Hegstrom

Gabor Maté

The Society of NLP

Dr. David Hawkins

Bruce D. Schneider

The Institute for Professional Excellence in
    Coaching (iPEC)

Esther Hicks (aka Abraham Hicks)

Keven, Cherie, Thach & EnMay

Jim Shaffer

and Jane

And a heartfelt thank you to Goran Mrvic for pulling this content out of me. To Rachel Paling for consistently pushing me to new heights and demanding more from me. To Penny Roberts for unequivocally helping me to the nth degree. To my beta readers for each and every adjustment you made that created the perfect read. To my book designing and editing team, know that I would be lost without you. And lastly to my family and my amazing kids for allowing me the time and space to make it happen. Your presence was wholeheartedly noted. Namaste.

Key Terms

action, outcome & behavior: the end result and/or compound effect of the values, beliefs, stories, thoughts and emotions collectively experienced; the expression of

Alfred Korzybski: the founder of the semantic expression, the map is not the territory

anchor: any previously experienced internal memory that is engaged by an internal and/or external trigger/ representation system that is similar to the original experience

anxiety: the experience of anxious emotions

arrested emotional development: occurs when an emotion is seized in development and remains in that contracted state as the rest of the emotions develop at their natural pace; AED

awareness: having conscious knowledge that something is or has occurred

auditory: to hear

behaviors: the way in which a person conducts themself in accordance with their surroundings

beliefs: simply a framework of ideas that one has deemed true

childhood trauma: the presence and/or experience of adverse childhood experiences that occur before eighteen years of age

coherence: the state of wholeness; calm, solid, grounded, positive energy; unfragmented

confirmation bias: the act of searching for evidence that supports one's position

consciousness: the complete awareness of what one is experiencing

conscious middle: the middle section where there is an equal distribution of anabolic energy and catabolic energy, creating an opportunity for either to increase

developmental trauma: the continual presence of trauma that interrupts the developmental process of childhood

Dissociated Healing™: a modality that allows people to dissociate from their present-day self, used to heal previous traumas

emotional development: the stages in which a person develops emotionally, learning what emotions are, understanding how to feel feelings, how to process feelings and how to release feelings

emotional dysregulation: the interrupted and/or seized stages of emotional development

emotional regulation: the ability to control your emotional state

emotions: the mental reaction that evokes feelings

energy: the application of force conveyed consciously or unconsciously

entrainment: the cadence that occurs in response to and in alignment with one's environment, physically, mentally and emotionally

equanimity: the ability to remain calm and unfazed even in the most tumultuous of situations, remaining focused on an intentional, internal state that maintains one's connection to oneself

gustatory: to taste

imprinting: when the impact of a first experience leaves a deep, lasting impression and then later becoming precedent for that specific individual

Intentional Consciousness™: the act of intentionally choosing the state of mind to engage in said

Interrupt the Story™: the action of using the acronym STOP to interrupt a current pattern. (STOP: Story versus serve, Truth big *T* versus little *t*, Opportunities versus options, Power versus possibilities)

KAVOG: acronym for kinesthetic, auditory, visual, olfactory, gustatory

kinesthetic: to feel

LOE: acronym for level of energy

map: the personal collection of experiences that each individual houses

mask: the facade that one hides behind

NLP: acronym for neuro linguistic programming

NeuroEnlighten™ method: a healing method used to create awareness and to acknowledge and release rooted, and often unconscious, memories from the nervous system

OFP: acronym for over-functioning parent

olfactory: to smell

over-functioning: occurs when someone offers unwarranted energy in hopes of helping, serving, fixing or changing another without their request and/or consent

psychological sunburn: the volatile response that comes when energy is directed into an unknown and open, psychological wound

representational systems: the five senses often referred to in NLP

Scissor Syndrome™: the position that an over-functioning person engages in while attempting to help, serve, fix or change others

shadow: the residual pieces of a previous version of you that still currently linger in your energy

Six Layers of Human Behavior™: values, beliefs, stories, thoughts, emotions, actions, outcomes & behaviors

SMEEPS: acronym for the six areas that energy is influenced by, including social, mental, emotional, environmental, physical and spiritual

state: the level of emotion and/or mood one is experiencing

strategy: a series of decisions one makes to produce a consistent outcome

stories: the culmination of past experiences, ideas, values, beliefs, thoughts emotions and levels of energy

TEA: acronym for thought, emotion, action (also action, outcome and behavior)

TEA Loops™: the TEA process followed by the presence of confirmation bias, which returns loops one back to the initial thought, creating a cyclical response

thoughts: an idea that emanates from a story

territory: the area that is available to experience as a whole (the world)

trauma: any experience that takes one outside of coherence; anything that engages a fight or flight response

trauma response: the unconscious response to the ongoing, deeply embedded, normalized presence of trauma

trigger: the action that engages one's emotional response

UFP: acronym for under-functioning parent

unconscious mind: the area of your mind that runs on default, without conscious awareness and/or choice

under-functioning: the action of negating and/or neglecting responsibilities; not being emotionally, physically or mentally available; procrastinating

values: the high standard concepts that one deems important

visual: to see

Bibliography

American Psychiatric Association. *Diagnostic and Statistical Manual of Mental Disorders: DSM-IV-TR.* 4th ed. Washington, DC: American Psychiatric Association, 2000.

Bandler, Richard. "Anchoring: Accessing and Re-Accessing Representations." In *Charisma Enhancement™ & Trainer Training Manual*, edited by John La Valle, 20–23. The Society of NLP, 1994.

Bandler, Richard. *Richard Bandler's Guide to Trance-Formation: Make Your Life Great.* London: HarperElement, 2010.

Bandler, Richard. *Time for a Change.* Cupertino, Calif.: Meta Publications, 1993.

Bandler, Richard, Glenda Bradstock, and Owen Fitzpatrick. *Thinking on Purpose: A 15-Day Plan to a Smarter Life.* Hopatcong, NJ: New Thinking Publications, 2019.

Bandler, Richard, and John Grinder. *The Structure of Magic. A Book about Communication and Change.* Palo Alto, Calif.: Science & Behavior Books, 1976.

Berger, David. *If You Can Feel It You Can Heal It.* Scotts Valley, Calif.: CreateSpace Publishing, 2012.

Colan, Lee. "A Lesson from Roy A. Disney on Making Values-Based Decisions." Inc.com. Accessed July 14, 2022, https://www.inc.

com/lee-colan/a-lesson-from-roy-a-disney-on-making-values-based-decisions.html.

De Bellis, Michael D., and Abigail Zisk. "The Biological Effects of Childhood Trauma." *Child and Adolescent Psychiatric Clinics of North America 23* (2): 185–222, April 2014. https://doi.org/10.1016/j.chc.2014.01.002

Dispenza, Joe. *Breaking the Habit of Being Yourself: How to Lose Your Mind and Create a New One*. Carlsbad, Calif.: Hay House, 2018.

Dodson, Frederick. *Increase Your Energy*. [S.I.]: Lulu.com, 2021.

Dyer, Wayne W. *The Power of Intention: Learning to Co-Create Your World Your Way*. Carlsbad, Calif.: Hay House, 2012.

English, Horace B., and Ava C. English. *A Comprehensive Dictionary of Psychological and Psychoanalytical Terms: A Guide to Usage*. Taiwan: Longmans, Green, 1958.

Hawkins, David R. *Power vs. Force: The Hidden Determinants of Human Behavior*. Carlsbad, Calif.: Hay House, 2014.

Hawkins, David R. *The Eye of the I: From Which Nothing Is Hidden*. Carlsbad, Calif.: Hay House, 2016.

Hay House. "Manifesting Your Soul's Purpose with Dr. Wayne Dyer." n.d., accessed May 15, 2022, https://youtu.be/4nIAwUJv2Eo.

Hay, Louise L. *You Can Heal Your Life*. Carlsbad, Calif.: Hay House, 2008.

HeartMath Institute. "The Resilient Heart™: Trauma-Sensitive HeartMath Certification." HeartMath Institute. Accessed May 15, 2021. https://www.heartmath.com/certification/the-resilient-heart-trauma-sensitive-heartmath-certification/

Hegstrom, Paul. *Broken Children, Grown-up Pain: Understanding the Effects of Your Wounded Past*. Kansas City, Missouri: Beacon Hill Press, 2006.

Hicks, Esther, and Jerry Hicks. *Ask and It Is Given: Learning to Manifest Your Desires*. New Delhi, India: Hay House Publications (India) Pvt. Ltd, 2017.

Hill, Napoleon. *Think and Grow Rich*. Wise, Virginia: Napoleon Hill Foundation, 1989.

Jewel. *Never Broken: Songs Are Only Half the Story.* New York: Blue Rider Press, an imprint of Penguin Random House, 2016.

Jewel. "Never Broken" presented online as part of "The Wisdom of Trauma" Lecture Series. Accessed July 5, 2021, https://www.scienceandnonduality.com/.

Korzybski, Alfred, and Robert P. Pula. *Science and Sanity: An Introduction to Non-Aristotelian Systems and General Semantics.* Fort Worth, Tx.: Institute of General Semantics, 2005.

Lapierre, Aline, and Laurence Heller. *Healing Developmental Trauma.* Berkley, Calif.: North Atlantic Books, 2012.

Maté, Gabor. *In the Realm of Hungry Ghosts: Close Encounters with Addiction.* London: Vermillion, an imprint of Ebury Publishing, 2018.

Maté, Gabor, and Daniel Maté. *The Myth of Normal.* London: Vermillion, an imprint of Ebury Publishing, 2018.

Maté, Gabor. "The Wisdom of Trauma" Lecture Series, March 4-7, 2021. Accessed July 5, 2021, https://www.scienceandnonduality.com/.

Nhất Hạnh, and Robert Ellsberg. *The Essential Thich Nhat Hanh: Thich Nhat Hanh.* London: Darton Longman & Todd, 2008.

Oxford English Dictionary Online. OED.com. Accessed July 26, 2022, http://www.oed.com/viewdictionaryentry/Entry/11125.

Schneider, Bruce. *Institute for Professional Excellence in Coaching iPEC Manual.* Chicago: IL, 2019.

Starr Commonwealth. "Children of Trauma & Resilience." Starr Commonwealth online course, October 8, 2019. Accessed December 30, 2021, https://starr.org/our-courses/.

van der Kolk, Bessel. *The Body Keeps the Score: Mind, Brain and Body in the Transformation of Trauma.* London: Penguin Books, 2015.

Watts, Alan. "Exploring Your Dark Side." Alan Watts Organization. Accessed March 3, 2022, https://youtu.be/32MiAPR2S4g.

Unknown. "Values Development." Changingminds.org. Accessed April 3, 2020, https://changingminds.org/explanations/values/values_development.htm

Endnotes

Chapter 1

1. Korzybski, *Science and Sanity*, 2005.

Chapter 3

2. Jewel, *Never Broken*, 2016.
3. Watts, "Exploring Your Dark Side," accessed, March 3, 2022.
4. Dispenza, *Breaking the Habit of Being Yourself*, 2018.
5. Lapierre and Heller, *Healing Developmental Trauma*, 2012.

Chapter 4

6. Berger, *If You Can Feel It You Can Heal It*, 2012.

Chapter 6

7. Hill, *Think and Grow Rich*, 1989.
8. Taken from a presentation given by Dr. Rao Kolusu and Jodee Gibson titled "Understanding Human Behavior" on March 7, 2021.

Chapter 7

9. Bandler, "Anchoring: Accessing and Re-Accessing Representations," 1994.
10. Bandler, *Richard Bandler's Guide to Trance-Formation*, 2010.
11. Bandler, "Anchoring: Accessing and Re-Accessing Representations," 1994.
12. Taken from NLP Master Practitioner Training held in London, England on July 14, 2018, and a subsequent personal conversation between Kathleen La Valle and Jodee Gibson.
13. Bandler, *Time for a Change*, 1993.
14. Bandler, *Time for a Change*, 1993.
15. Unknown, "Value Development," Changingminds.org, accessed April 3, 2020.
16. Colan, "A Lesson from Roy Disney," Inc.com, accessed July 14, 2022.
17. Taken from a personal conversation between John La Valle and Jodee Gibson during an NLP training conference held on July 14, 2018.
18. Bandler, "Anchoring: Accessing and Re-Accessing Representations," 1994.

Chapter 8

19. Bandler, Bradstock, and Fitzpatrick, *Thinking on Purpose*, 2019.

Chapter 9

20. Hawkins, *Power vs Force*, 2014.
21. Hawkins, *The Eye of the I,* 2016.
22. Hill, *Think and Grow Rich*, 1989.
23. Schneider, *Institute for Professional Excellence in Coaching Manual*, 2019.
24. Hawkins, *Power vs Force*, 2014.
25. Hawkins, *Power vs Force*, 2014.
26. Dodson, *Increase Your Energy*, 2021.
27. Hicks, *Ask and It Is Given*, 2017.
28. Schneider, *Institute for Professional Excellence in Coaching Manual*, 2019.

29. Dyer, *Power of Intention*, 2012.
30. Hay House, "Manifesting Your Soul's Purpose," Accessed May 15, 2022.

Chapter 10

31. Bandler, "Anchoring: Accessing and Re-Accessing Representations," 1994.
32. Schneider, *Institute for Professional Excellence in Coaching Manual*, 2019.

Chapter 11

33. Hay, *You Can Heal Your Life*, 2008.
34. Nhat Hanh and Ellsberg, *The Essential Thich Nhat Hanh*, 2008.

Chapter 12

35. van der Kolk, *The Body Keeps the Score*, 2015.
36. Bandler, *Richard Bandler's Guide to Trance-Formation*, 2010.
37. Dyer, *Power of Intention*, 2012.

Chapter 13

38. Hegstrom, *Broken Children, Grown-Up Pain*, 2006.
39. van der Kolk, *The Body Keeps the Score*, 2015.
40. van der Kolk, *The Body Keeps the Score*, 2015.
41. Maté, *In the Realm of Hungry Ghosts*, 2018.
42. Starr Commonwealth, "Children of Trauma & Resilience," October 8, 2019.
43. HeartMath Institute, "The Resilient Heart," May 15, 2021.
44. Maté, *The Myth of Normal*, 2018.
45. Maté, "The Wisdom of Trauma," 2021.
46. American Psychiatric Association, *Diagnostic and Statistical Manual of Mental Disorders*, 2000.
47. Starr Commonwealth, "Children of Trauma & Resilience," October 8, 2019.
48. Starr Commonwealth, "Children of Trauma & Resilience," October 8, 2019.
49. Hegstrom, *Broken Children, Grown-Up Pain*, 2006.

HEALING YOUR MAP

50. van der Kolk, *The Body Keeps the Score*, 2015.
51. English, *Comprehensive Dictionary of Psychological and Psychoanalytical Terms*, 1958.
52. De Bellis and Zisk, "The Biological Effects of Childhood Trauma," 185–222.
53. Oxford English Dictionary Online
54. Dyer, *The Power of Intention*, 2012.
55. Hawkins, *Power vs Force*, 2014.
56. Schneider, *Institute for Professional Excellence in Coaching iPEC Manual*, 2019.
57. Taken from a personal conversation between Owen Fitzpatrick and Jodee Gibson on June 1, 2022.
58. Jewel, *Never Broken*, 2016.

About the Author

As a native Detroiter, Jodee refused to be marginalized by her early experiences as a wildly uneducated teen mom. Choosing to defy the odds, she blazed a new path fueled by an insatiable quest for **personal development** and **self-mastery.** Jodee emerged from her experiences as a multifaceted leader, deeply educated in human behavior, both formally and experientially. Her unconventional approach to helping people heal from past trauma and live their best life is something every person on the planet deserves to learn. Although Jodee may be considered a human behavior expert, she will forever remain a student of this work. If her transformational journey piques your interest, visit here to learn more:

WWW.JODEEGIBSON.COM

Please leave a review!

For a self-published author like myself, reviews mean the world! Please leave a review on Amazon, Google, or other on-line retailer. Tell me what you really thought—be honest! Either good or bad, I'd like to know.

Thank you so much for purchasing my book!

REVIEW ON

AND OTHER ONLINE RETAILERS

Made in the USA
Las Vegas, NV
30 October 2022

58454318R00195